BALLOT BOXING

BALLOT BOXING

DEMOCRACY IS ONLY AS STRONG AS ITS VOTERS

LUCY SANTORA

NEW DEGREE PRESS

COPYRIGHT © 2021 LUCY SANTORA

BALLOT BOXING

Democracy Is Only as Strong as Its Voters

ISBN   978-1-63730-713-7   *Paperback*
          978-1-63730-851-6   *Kindle Ebook*
          979-8-88504-002-0   *Ebook*

For my mom, who taught me to embrace entropy as an opportunity for my next great adventure.

CONTENTS

*Democracy is not a spectator sport; it is
a participatory event. If we do not participate
in it, it ceases to be a democracy.*

—MICHAEL MOORE

INTRODUCTION

I'll never forget jumping on Avery's trampoline in late 2008. We were childhood friends, the kind you have because your families put you in the same place at the same time, nothing deeper. Just kids who didn't know how different we were from one another. But like all forms of childhood innocence, that too would change. I had just told her my parents had voted early for Barack Obama. It was like I had just informed her that Santa, the tooth fairy, and the Easter bunny were not real. Her eyes got wide, and she whispered, "Why would they do that? Obama is the Antichrist." At that very moment, our parents were a few streets over at their weekly Bible study. Avery also thought that Catholics weren't real Christians, so I was only half-listening to her anyway.

But that night, I went home and asked my mom about it.

She laughed and told me people were very polarized over this election and "people demonize what they fear." I didn't think about that moment for a long time, but it's my earliest memory of politics.

If you found the 2020 election emotionally exhausting, feel overwhelmed by the twenty-four-hour news cycle, or can't find the time to figure out what is going on in American politics right now, this is the book for you. There's so much information out there, and even the best reporting can feel biased or too highbrow. This journey is nonpartisan, pro-voter, and brutally honest. My only agenda is to show you why your vote is essential to the American democratic experiment and that you should exercise that right frequently and consistently.

I spent my entire childhood in a red brick house in a suburb of Dallas, Texas. Everyone went to church on Sunday and voted straight-Republican tickets. Except for my parents. My mom is from Connecticut, and my father is from Massachusetts. They moved to the Lone Star state a few weeks before I was born for my father's job. We're Italian American and Roman Catholic. My mom is very open minded, and my father is fiscally conservative. This combination made for a confusing upbringing.

Mass on Sundays for me was a series of sit, stand, kneel repeat, and when I went to church with my non-denominational friends, it was Christian rock music with donuts and coffee. I was always confused why the people who went on mission trips to New Orleans and South Texas in the summer voted against government social programs in the fall.

The same people with the Ten Commandments hanging in their bathroom would steal political signs from our lawn in the middle of the night. We had an Obama sign in our yard, and within two days of it being out, it was stolen. My mom put another one out; that too was stolen. My dad wanted to set up a camera to determine who was taking the signs; my mom had a different approach. She ordered at least sixty Obama yard signs, one for every day until the election. Each morning she would walk outside and put a new one in the front yard, and each night someone would steal it. Naively, I thought this was hilarious. *It's a stupid sign; why would someone put so much energy into taking it.* I would be eating peanut butter toast before school, and my mom would be hammering the new sign into the ground.

Today I recognize how that was a violation of our First Amendment rights, especially when all of the houses around us were decked out in McCain signs. I asked my mom why they took our signs, and again she said, "People demonize what they fear."

My parents never pushed their political ideology onto me. They always promoted critical thinking. When I was in elementary school, we had an influx of new students as their families were relocated in the wake of Hurricane Katrina. In my young mind, I saw that the government had built them their neighborhood. Quickly I learned it was called Section 8 housing, and the neighborhood parents had mixed feelings. We had a school supply and holiday drive for the new families, but I heard the adults say their presence would decrease the property values of the surrounding area. To be fair, my only concept of finances at this point was saving up tickets after softball games so we could go to the concession stand and get fun dip. My mom always promoted giving; I think that's why I thought it was so simple: If people need help, then help them.

Nothing is that simple. When I asked my mom why the influx of new families was controversial, she told me, "Some people only want change they can control." Only years later, I put together how the sudden arrival of people from New Orleans would be upsetting to our suburban community.

Middle school came with an extra serving of sass, and I became fed up with the non-answers from my parents. If I asked about Section 8 housing, tax cuts, or war in Afghanistan, my mom would say, "Well, what do you think?" I was so annoyed. "Well, Catherine's parents think we should reduce food stamp accessibility, and Avery's parents agree, but I know you don't, so what's the right answer?" Every time, she responded, "Well, what do you think, Lucy?" Of course, my Catholic upbringing ingrained in me that we should always help the less fortunate, but seeing other Christians (who had more Bible verses memorized than I could count) vehemently stand against such measures stuck with me. I was old enough to know it wasn't that simple, but still too young to ascertain exactly what was making it so complicated. My parents didn't tell me what to think, so I had to draw my own conclusions. Today, I am grateful they forced me to do so. It compelled me to listen and try to understand the why behind my friends' voting habits.

Receiving my first ballot in 2016 was so exciting. I finally had the chance to participate in how my country would be run. I was voting absentee from Los Angeles as a student at the University of Southern California. So many people thought I was going to turn into a "crazy liberal" with blue hair. If anything, I'd say I belong to the radical middle, an independent who makes decisions based on what I think is best for the country and my community—not party lines or a single issue.

Looking at my ballot, I saw it was much longer than I expected; there were so many positions to vote for—railroad commissioner? What the hell is a comptroller? I was up until three in the morning researching candidates and trying to figure out what they stood for and if they should receive my vote. It was exhausting. Rolling into class the next day, I had dark circles under my eyes. My friend Shreya asked if I was trying to finish an essay. "No, trying to figure out what the hell the railroad commissioner does and how that affects the Twenty-Fourth District of Texas." Sharing that in Texas we vote for railroad commissioners and sheriffs while standing in front of her in cowboy boots and a sundress must have been a striking image for Shreya, a San Francisco native. I think she was trying to figure out my political ideology—the cowboy boots must have screamed Republican—but parents from the East Coast signaled Democrat. She never asked me point blank whom I voted for, but I think she figured it out pretty quickly.

Four years later, I was thoroughly obsessed with the 2020 election. The prospect of Texas flipping blue was enthralling; money poured in from around the nation, and people mobilized like never before. I applied for my absentee ballot in August, doing everything I could to ensure my vote was counted.

September came and went, no ballot. October came, and friends voting absentee were receiving their ballots. I reached out to all of the other students I knew in Los Angeles who were voting absentee for Texas. My friends who were registered Republicans had received their ballots; my friends registered Democrat had not. I was registered as an Independent. Now, this was a small sample size and there was a lot of buzz around stealing the election, but I tried not to drink the Kool-Aid. The election had become a sticky maze of theories about malware in voting machines, ballots made from bamboo being flown in from China, dead people voting, and suspicious hiccups that tried to defy reason and logic. This noise would only get louder, but we didn't know that yet.

Eventually, I found myself on the phone with the voting office for the Twenty-Fourth District of Texas every day asking about my ballot. I wasn't the only one with this problem, and an exasperated employee sighed on the other end and told me, "You'll get it before the election." I did get my ballot before the election—November 2, to be exact. I filled it out and ran to the post office. Thankfully, the marvelous US Postal Service confirmed it got there in under twenty-four hours, though I have no confirmation whether my vote was counted.

Too much of my energy was going into this election. I stayed up all night watching the votes come in, flipping between Fox News and CNN while frantically scrolling Twitter. The focus was on districts and states flipping blue or red, and my brain was overwhelmed with constantly changing numbers as the votes came in. The vote-counting disputes were well underway when I started to wonder if flipping states and districts were the most important story of the electorate. What so many people—myself included—missed was that the story of polarization wasn't about red to blue, but instead the shades of those two colors.

If you start looking for patterns, you find them in unexpected places. While putting my third bag of Skinny Pop into the microwave (which defeats the purpose, I know), I realized a connection. Madison Cawthorn (R-NC 11) and Alexandria Ocasio-Cortez (D-NY 14) have one key thing in common. They both won primaries where they were the challenger to the establishment. Neither flipped districts, but they moved safe blue and deep red areas further from the center. Between handfuls of exploded corn, my mind started to race, the zigzagging that only a morning person up way past her self-imposed bedtime could entertain. Voters first flocked to Trump because he wasn't a political insider and spoke like he was talking to an old friend at a bar, not with carefully calculated rhetoric. Maybe this phenomenon isn't exclusive to the Donald. Now more than ever, people want to see themselves in their politicians.

Right and left have fallen into polarized factions; their only unifying factor is a disdain for the other side. My mom was right; people do demonize what they fear. Republicans are afraid of progressive policies that will increase taxes, and thus they spew nonsensical hatred on the *Tucker Carlson Show*. In turn, Democrats fear inequality that leads to civil rights backsliding and therefore fight back on their networks. In the middle of this mess is the American voter, torn between two sides and often presented with no good choices. The grand political canyon reinforces this hyper-partisan landscape, leaving us voters with no option other than to pick sides.

Growing up in a blue house in a red state forced me to see both sides. I couldn't demonize either political party because one was my parents and the other my friends and neighbors. I've seen devout Christians vote against social programs, progressive friends turn into leftists, lifetime Republicans support universal health care, and wealthy liberals bemoan tax increases. My experience is the complex reality of American politics. Not even at university, where many young Americans find political solace, could I retreat to a partisan bubble. Conservatives saw the girl from Texas as an ally; the liberals saw a mind to be changed. Ultimately, I was neither.

Of course, I have strong opinions on what is best for this country, but I recognize that where you're from and who you've known deeply affect how you vote. I do not fear the fringes of our society; I fear the rest of us are complacent and accept this division. I fear we do not truly value the marvel of voting in a free society. I fear many of us vote without thinking or think without voting. Do I demonize the non-voter or the straight-ticket voter? I try desperately not to because I believe they can still be saved. Maybe it is the Catholic in me or the stubbornness of a born and raised Texan, but I'm not willing to wait any longer. We must come to terms with the state of American politics today and protect our future as a nation.

Together, we'll explore the history of voting rights and trends that shaped the landscape we face today, examine cases that illuminate the political divide in the United States, and present ideas on how everyday people can take charge of what happens in their communities that affect voter outcomes. This is your country, your community, your home, and you don't have to be a high-roller donor or political nut to hold power. I will show how you—the individual—have the ultimate control over our democracy.

PART 1

HOW WE GOT HERE

CHAPTER 1

CRASH COURSE IN THE HISTORY OF VOTING RIGHTS IN AMERICA

The history of voting rights in the United States is intrinsically tied to the nation's struggle for women and people of color to have the same voice as a property-owning white man. Women have only been able to vote in this country for one hundred years, and the voting rights of people of color have only been protected for fifty-five years. For the self-proclaimed world's greatest democracy, we've only had voting equity for 20 percent of our 245 years. If the 2020 election taught us anything, it's that voting is still complicated and controversial. Looking back, it makes sense how we got here, and why there is work still left to be done.

1870—THE FIFTEENTH AMENDMENT

The year 1870 brought the passing of the Fifteenth Amendment, which technically gave black men the right to vote: "The right of citizens of the United States to vote shall not be denied or abridged by the United States or by any State on account of race, color, or previous condition of servitude." The critical loophole is that states couldn't stop people from voting based on three things—race, color, if they had been slaves—but states could find other means to mute the black vote. After the Fifth Amendment, literacy tests and poll taxes became required to vote in many states, specifically targeting the black community, many of whom had little education or money due to the legacy of slavery. Such barriers to voting were the antithesis of a free democracy. One test in Mississippi was particularly egregious: Prospective voters had to transcribe and interpret a section of the state constitution and write an essay on their duty as a citizen of the nation. Polling officials would then read the tests and decide who passed, effectively hand-selecting who would get to vote. Leaders in the South knew if they could find ways around the amendment and decide whose vote counted, they could effectively control the outcome of every election in their state.

When the United States passed the Fifteenth Amendment, there were three black members of Congress: Jefferson Franklin Long, Rainey Joseph Hayne, and Hiram Rhodes Revels. Long spoke out against the Amnesty Bill, which restored political rights to former confederates. He was the first black person to speak on the House floor. The House of Representative archives quote him saying, "Do we, then, really propose here today . . . to relieve from political disability the very men who have committed these Ku Klux outrages? I think that I am doing my duty to my constituents and my duty to my country when

I vote against such a proposition." Looking back from the twenty-first century, I find it disturbing how quickly confederates' voting rights were restored, almost as fast as the United States withheld those same rights from black men. It gives insight into what defined "healing the nation." Healing meant giving white men back their privileges as citizens, not forcefully bringing the country together as one people.

1920—WOMEN GAIN THE RIGHT TO VOTE

The Nineteenth Amendment was first introduced in Congress in 1878, but not ratified until 1920. It states in plain language, "The right of citizens of the United States to vote shall not be denied or abridged by the United States or by any State on account of sex."

Note: The amendment specifies sex, not race. Women of color were not included in this breakthrough, despite being an intrinsic part of the suffragist movement. In 1866, Elizabeth Cady Stanton, Susan B. Anthony, and Frederick Douglass formed the American Equal Rights Association, advocating for suffrage for all Americans regardless of sex or race. It had only been a year since the Civil War ended, and the moment was ripe for healing, but Reconstruction and equality were not an easy pairing. It would take almost a century after black men were given the right to vote for them to be able to exercise it without significant barriers.

The 1960s were fraught with racial tension. Maybe it was orators like Martin Luther King Jr., or the Black Panthers and Bobby Seale, or perhaps the Howard University Students protesting in the streets—but this time, change happened. My grandmother grew up in a country where black men fought in both World Wars, Vietnam, and Korea, but were asked to write an essay about the duties of citizenship before casting a ballot. She watched King's "I Have a Dream" speech in real time, while I witnessed it as a grainy black-and-white video in social studies class. I was quizzed on the Civil Rights Acts; my grandmother saw them become law. In just over a generation, monumental progress became school curriculum.

The 1964 Act outlawed discrimination based on race, color, religion, sex, or national origin. The 1968 Act made it illegal to refuse to sell or rent to any person based on anything other than their financial resources. And 1965, that was the one I always remembered, the Voting Rights Act. The 1965 Voting Rights Act gave non-white people their Fifteenth Amendment rights. Section 2 of the act, titled Congressional Purpose and Findings, states, "The purpose of this act is to ensure that the right of all citizens to vote, including the right to register to vote and cast meaningful votes, is preserved and protected as guaranteed by the Constitution."

While the Voting Rights Act didn't fix everything, it drastically changed the electorate. According to a 2019 report by Danyelle Solomon on systematic inequality, from 1965 to 1968, the number of black citizens registered to vote in Alabama, Georgia, and Louisiana doubled, and Mississippi saw black voter registration increase tenfold. More black citizens voting meant more black representation in Congress. The report also details that in 1970, there were 1,469 black elected officials in the United States, and by 1980, it had tripled to 4,912. Later amendments to the act required jurisdictions to provide translated voting materials for Americans with limited English proficiency (LEP) if the LEP population was greater than 10,000 or constituted more than 5 percent of the voting population. These provisions have greatly assisted Latino Americans and Asian Americans in participating in our democracy.

2010S—BACKSLIDING

At the dawn of the twenty-first century, state legislators had become more subtle with their efforts to choose their electorate. In 2011 and 2012, eight states introduced bills to restrict voter registration drives. These states weren't all red or blue; they included California, Florida, Illinois, Michigan, Mississippi, Nevada, North Carolina, and South Carolina. The Brennan Center for Justice recorded one Florida state senator's reasoning in a 2011 memo. Senator Bennett said, "We do make it convenient for people to vote, but I gotta tell ya I wouldn't even have any problem making it harder. . . . I want the people in the State of Florida to want to vote as badly as that person in Africa who is willing to walk 200 miles for that opportunity he's never had before in his life. This should not be easy."

The resurgence of attempts to suppress voters in 2011 and 2012 was not a coincidence. The country was gearing up for a presidential election, an election where it would be determined if the first black president, Barack Obama, would receive a second term. Bumper stickers read, "If you voted for him the first time to prove you're not racist, vote against him now to prove you're not stupid." While undoubtedly some people didn't vote for Obama because of his race, others disagreed with his policies. Those bumper stickers eventually disappeared, and 2012 marked the first time the national voter turnout rate among black citizens exceeded that of white citizens. Obama won a second term.

This moment is where pieces of the puzzle start to shift into place to show us the landscape of the 2020 elections. The Supreme Court decision in *Shelby County v. Holder* made Section 5 of the Voting Rights Act unenforceable, meaning states could alter their voting policies without seeking federal approval.

Shelby v. Holder completely changed the trajectory of voting rights in the United States. The case brought decades of incremental progress to a halt. Shelby County, Alabama, was the petitioner and filed the suit in a district court claiming Section 5 and Section 4b of the Voting Rights Act of 1965 were unconstitutional. Junior attorney general Eric Holder wrote the judgment, and the court ruled these sections were constitutional. Appeals were made, and the case made its way through the justice system until it reached the Supreme Court. The legal question:

Does the renewal of Section 5 of the Voter Rights Act under the constraints of Section 4b exceed Congress' authority under the Fourteenth and Fifteenth Amendments, and therefore violate the Tenth Amendment and Article 4 of the Constitution?

Let's break this down:

- Tenth Amendment: Powers not delegated to the United States by the Constitution, nor prohibited by it to the States, are reserved to the States, respectively
- Fourteenth Amendment: Grants citizenship to everyone born or naturalized in the United States
- Fifteenth Amendment: The right of citizens to vote will not be denied based on race, color, or previous condition of servitude
- Voting Rights Act of 1965
    - Section 4: Determines the states and localities that Section 5 will cover
    - Section 5: Jurisdictions with a history of discrimination must obtain federal approval before changing voting rules

Thus the question becomes:

Does Congress have the power to continue to make historically discriminatory jurisdictions obtain federal approval before changing voting rules? Or does this go beyond the protections of citizens voting rights? According to the Tenth Amendment, changing voting rules should be left up to the states if it goes beyond said powers.

The Supreme Court ruled that Section 4 of the Voting Rights Act is unconstitutional. Chief Justice John G. Roberts Jr. wrote the majority opinion making three main points:

1. "Section 5 of the Act required States to obtain federal permission before enacting any law related to voting—a drastic departure from the basic principles of federalism."
2. "And [Section] 4 of the Act applied that requirement only to some States—an equally dramatic departure from the principle that all States enjoy equal sovereignty."
3. "There is no denying, however, that the conditions that originally justified these measures no longer characterize voting in the covered jurisdictions."

Justice Ruth Bader Ginsburg wrote the dissent highlighting two critical reasons to keep the sections in effect:

4. "Continuance would facilitate completion of the impressive gains thus far made."
5. "Continuance would guard against backsliding."

Justice Ginsberg was right; backsliding began shortly after the Supreme Court made the ruling. North Carolina quickly added a law that required voters to present a state-issued photo ID, cut early voting days, banned same-day voter registration, added new restrictions on casting provisional ballots, and prohibited pre-registration for sixteen- and seventeen-year-olds. PBS *Frontline* reported that this was overturned in 2016 when a federal appeals court said, "With race data in hand, the legislature amended the bill to exclude many of the alternative photo IDs used by African Americans. As amended, the bill retained only the kinds of IDs that white North Carolinians were more likely to possess."

In the same year North Dakota adopted a voter ID law that required citizens to present an ID with a valid residential street address to vote. This law clearly targeted Native Americans, many of whom lived on reservations without residential addresses. One in five otherwise eligible Native Americans in North Dakota were affected by this law.

2020—NEW RULES

2020 was an unprecedented election year for numerous reasons, one of the most glaring that it was happening during the COVID-19 pandemic. America had voted during a pandemic before, in the 1918 midterm elections. Back then, candidates campaigned via newspapers and written pamphlets instead of rallies, and people went to the polls in masks. However, some poll sites couldn't open because there weren't enough healthy people in the area to run them, and politicians accused each other of suppressing the vote. Sound familiar?

More than one hundred years later, the country faced almost the same problem, with some technological differences.

For example, Indiana passed Senate Bill 334, which created a system to crosscheck voter registrations to ensure their constituents weren't registered in another state and allowed counties to remove voters from their rolls without warning. Unfortunately, crosschecking often leads to errors since many people share the same name and move from one state to another. Removals without warning turned this bill into a voter purge statute that directly violated the National Voter Registration Act.

Iowa began requiring early voters to provide identification before receiving ballots. If a voter gave incomplete or incorrect information when requesting an absentee ballot, the county auditor office had to contact them by phone and email rather than using existing data in the voter database. This rule means a single typo or administrative error could be used to suppress voting.

Kentucky overrode a gubernatorial veto to pass a new voter ID law, and Louisiana limited who could serve as a witness for an absentee ballot. Meanwhile, Oklahoma enacted a new requirement that voters have to get their absentee ballot notarized or include a photocopy of their ID. Requiring a notary is, in essence, a poll tax, since many people lack access to a copy machine and many notaries charge for their services.

Tennessee took a different approach: targeting voter registration drives. The state now requires voter registration applications to be submitted within fifteen days of a drive and prohibits retaining voter information for non-political purposes.

The actions of state legislatures either protect or restrict the right to vote. The best argument for protections lies in the Fourteenth and Fifteenth Amendments. Meanwhile, the best argument for restrictions is fear over election tampering and fraudulent ballots.

The Cybersecurity and Infrastructure Security Agency (CISA) has an entire section of its website, called #Protect2020, that is dedicated to election security and disinformation surrounding the 2020 election. It explains the most common rumors and presents the facts, such as:

- Reality: Ballot handling procedures protect against intentional or unintentional ballot destruction
- Rumor: Ballots can easily be destroyed without detection, preventing them from being counted

Multiple agencies and politicians stated that the 2020 election was the most secure in history, and just as many voices have proclaimed the exact opposite. The 2020 election has probably been talked about and investigated more than any other election in our nation's history.

Recent memory might conjure images of hanging chads that became a symbol in the 2000 election and the Supreme Court decision that ended the Florida recount. The *Bush v. Gore* decision on December 12 of that year ended the thirty-six days of turmoil over who would take the oval office. In his concession speech, Gore made his position clear: "I accept the finality of this outcome which will be ratified next Monday in the electoral college. And tonight, for the sake of our unity of the people and the strength of our democracy, I offer my concession." These words could not be more opposite from the claims of victory that Donald Trump expounded during his lame duck period from November 3 to January 20. The 2000 election was indeed contested, but nowhere near the magnitude and damage that 2020 unleashed. I would put 2000 in third place for the most contested US presidential election.

If we look beyond living memory and assess every election in this nation's history to see if any can put 2020 in second place, we'll find plenty of controversial moments. The presidential election of 1800 went to the House of Representatives because Jefferson and Burr tied in the electoral college vote. It's such a dramatic story that it appeared as a plot point in a Broadway musical more than 200 years later.

Other tumultuous campaigns include Abraham Lincoln's election in 1860 during the Civil War and the 1912 election in which Theodore Roosevelt started the Progressive Party after the Democrats denied him the nomination. But that campaign was even more memorable because Roosevelt was shot mid-speech yet finished speaking before seeking medical attention. In 1948, everyone thought Dewey would defeat Truman; the Chicago Tribune had already printed the headline "Dewey Defeats Truman" ready for the morning paper. While all of these were exciting, none was as destructive to our democracy than the 2020 election.

The only election that can hold a candle to 2020's chaos took place in 1876, when Democrat Samuel Tilden ran against Republican Rutherford B. Hayes. Tilden won the popular vote and led in the electoral college, but he didn't have the 185 electoral votes required to win at the time. Nineteen votes remained disputed from the Republican controlled states of Louisiana, Florida, and South Carolina. There were allegations of voter fraud, and Congress set up a special electoral commission to investigate. The process was agonizing, and the outcome wasn't decided until just two days before the inauguration. The fifteen-person commission of senators, members of Congress, and Supreme Court justices voted for Hayes eight to seven, granting him all the disputed electoral votes.

However, there was a distinct quid pro quo known as the Compromise of 1877. Democrats agreed to accept Hayes' victory so long as they removed federal troops from the former Confederate states, appointed a southern Democrat to Hayes' cabinet, constructed another transcontinental railroad through Texas and the South, passed legislation to help industrialize the South, and gave the South the right to deal with African American citizens in southern states without northern interference. As with any unofficial agreement, not all elements were delivered. The Hayes administration removed troops from the South, and Hayes did appoint a Democrat to his cabinet, but the legislation and new railroad never came to light. The final point of the agreement had been well underway prior but became enshrined and effectively ended Reconstruction, and white supremacists reclaimed power and started passing legislation to subjugate former slaves.

While the gravity of the civil rights implications is severe, the 1876 election only takes the silver medal. For all the setbacks of this election, the people's faith in their government and the government's faith in itself would be resolved. Our nation healed, shone, and prospered—until the 2020 election reopened these generational scars and eroded the people's trust in not just the United States government but the efficacy of democracy.

The American Bar Association documented that there have been over forty court cases challenging the 2020 election. Republicans filed these claims in five states that Biden won: Arizona, Georgia, Michigan, Nevada, and Pennsylvania, as well as direct appeals to the Supreme Court. Every single challenge failed:

- Three cases rejected by the Supreme Court
- Thirteen losses in Pennsylvania
- Four losses in Nevada
- Five failures in Georgia
- Five defeats in Michigan
- Four losses in Arizona
- Seven losses in Wisconsin
- One loss in New Mexico

Despite all of this, as of late 2021, an estimated fifty million Republicans believe the 2020 election was stolen from former President Donald Trump. In a country of 331 million people, that's more than 15 percent of the population.

The ability to vote for our representatives is the crux of democracy. Maybe you've lost faith in our system—its history is messy and its present isn't much cleaner—but your fellow citizens are fighting to make things right. And they need you to use your agency and vote in order to succeed.

"Our system is imperfect, and it will disenfranchise a portion of the population, gerrymander a slice, and sometimes contest your vote." That is a bleak outlook that I beg you not to fall victim to. The truth is you can only be disenfranchised, gerrymandered, and challenged if you choose not to vote. When you don't vote, you have no power over who takes office, and thus, the people elected might not protect your rights the same way someone you backed would have. I'm here to show you that as messy as our system is, it's still our system. We have the ultimate power to make the system work for us or change it altogether. But we can't do any of that unless you vote. Quite frankly, I don't care who you vote for; I would rather have a high voter turnout and my candidate lose than have a low voter turnout and my candidate win. Because a high voter turnout means democracy is working for the people, and the election results are the will of the people. That's the America I want. That's the next chapter in our voting history I'm asking you to help me write. And it starts now.

CHAPTER 2

THE RISE OF BETO O'ROURKE AND THE PEOPLE'S PAC

You may know Beto as the guy who lost to Ted Cruz. The loss was by a margin closer than any other Texas Democratic candidate in decades. You may remember him as the congressman from El Paso. If you're a member of the NRA, he's the guy who said during one of the debates, "Hell yes, we're going to take your AR-15, your AK-47." While the name Beto conjures different images depending on who you are and where you're from, he is emblematic of tumultuous change in the Lone Star state.

Beto O'Rourke was born in El Paso, Texas, in 1972. His hometown is in the westernmost part of Texas and is practically across the street from Juarez, Mexico. Simply being born in El Paso, his life would be intrinsically connected to the US-Mexico border and distant from typical politicians who ran big cities like Dallas and Houston. Beto was elected to his city council in 2005 and served until 2011. He set the bar higher and defeated the

Democratic incumbent in 2012 to become the representative for Texas' Sixteenth Congressional District. At this point, the only people who know his name live in the gerrymandered confines of that district. He's re-elected in 2014 and 2016, but still no political splash.

In 2018 Beto, the former boy band member turned congressman, decided he wanted a larger audience. He was determined to take on Ted Cruz for a seat in the United States Senate. If you're from Texas like me, you remember this moment. You might have thought Beto was totally off his rocker. Ted Cruz was the first Hispanic American to represent Texas in the Senate. He's been in office since 2013. In 2018, Cruz was a household name, a Texas staple like bluebonnets and barbecue. Then came Beto, walking over the horizon of his border town to meet with the folks in the rest of the state.

One of the first things that made Beto special was that he embraced being a small-town politician that didn't know the political rulebook forward and backward. From the beginning, he refused to run his Senate campaign like a typical race. He didn't use pollsters or political consultants. Instead, all of his fundraising went into direct outreach—people to people. He told the Dallas Morning News in a 2017 interview, "My heart is in it, I want to do this, I'm driven to do it, I'm not poll-testing it, I'm not consulting with consultants." None of that mattered to Beto. He would live-stream his road trips across the state, and soon young Democrats knew his Whataburger order and marked their calendars for when he would be in town. Beto visited all 254 counties in Texas, despite the majority of voters living in only eight of them. His bottom line consisted of two things: Talk to everyone and don't take money from PACs.

Meanwhile, Ted Cruz and his fellow Republicans were amused at most. To them, it was almost cute to see a novice politician go door to door asking for votes. That tune changed very quickly as the polls started showing Beto gaining traction. According to Fox News, he had larger crowds and fundraising totals that hit $10.4 million in the second quarter, double what Cruz was pulling in from supporters.

Then came a small townhall-like campaign event that went viral. Beto was asked a question and the answer he gave rocketed him to national attention. That attention led to then-President Trump announcing a rally in Texas for Cruz for fear of the Republicans losing the Senate seat.

A NowThis Politics video showed that a man in the audience asked, "I kind of wanted to know how you personally felt about how disrespectful it is like you have NFL players kneeling during the national anthems. I wanted to know if you found that disrespectful to our country, to our veterans, and anybody related to that. I find it incredibly frustrating that people seem to be okay with that."

Beto responds, "My short answer is no, I don't think it's disrespectful." Depending on where you personally fall on the kneel or not to kneel spectrum, that answer might grind your gears or incite subconscious applause. Beto's short answer was nothing new, and it aligned perfectly with what Democrats and social justice advocates had been saying since Kaepernick took his first knee. What Beto did next changed everything: the long answer.

He began, "You can feel as this young man does, you can feel as I do, you're every bit as American all the same." There wasn't accusation or disdain in his voice; you could tell he genuinely believed this in his soul. He then dipped into a brief history of peaceful protest in the United States, from John Lewis crossing the Edmund Pettus Bridge to Rosa Parks refusing to go to the back of the bus, to the freedom riders in the sixties and their ability to bring positive change to their communities. Beto shared how kneeling was these players' way of bringing attention to an important issue while the entire country's eyes are glued to their television screens. He closed, "I can think of nothing more American than to peacefully stand or take a knee for your rights, anytime, anywhere, anyplace. So thank you very much for asking that question."

I remember my first time watching this video. I can't remember which platform I saw it on, but my eyes were locked on the shaky cell phone footage, and I hung on to every word. He took one of the most controversial issues that year, kneeling during the anthem, and made it a moment of unity. It was not that he changed people's minds, but that for maybe the first time, there was an articulate and non-combative conversation about a topic that was tearing people apart.

The election's pace sped up very quickly after that. Donations to Beto's campaign flowed in from all around the country while Trump put aside his uneasy relationship with Ted Cruz to try and conjure up more Republican votes. For the first time in a very long time, the Texas Republican Party was terrified of losing a Senate race. Beto broke records, raising thirty-eight million dollars in the third quarter, the most any US Senate candidate had ever raised during this time frame. Texas, as the deep red state, seemed a lot more purple.

The Republicans were painfully aware they were falling behind, but by the time Cruz and Beto met for their October 16th debate in San Antonio, Cruz' team's internal polling showed his popularity increased. The shift was due to the Cruz campaign running negative ads about Beto being accepting of kneeling during the national anthem—an action massively unpopular in Texas at the time. However, the shift was spring-boarded by Brett Kavanaugh's nomination to the Supreme Court and subsequent hearings. That is the trouble with political campaigns. They never happen in a vacuum and can be easily sidetracked by external politics. Regardless of the allegations of sexual assault against Kavanaugh, many Republicans would vote for him since they badly wanted a conservative judge on the court. A desire for conservatism in the highest court in the land led many Republicans to rally behind Ted Cruz once again; every Senate seat would count when voting to confirm judges. Tension built, and at this point, it was practically palpable.

In moments like that, being a seasoned politician had advantages. Beto cracked. Or at least, that was how many saw his sudden shift in strategy. He discarded the persona of the boy band bass player, all grown up and trying to do good by his neighbors. Instead Beto became a man who had been kicked one too many times and was willing to fight fire with fire. Beto's campaign began running negative ads against Cruz, and Beto himself started dropping more bellicose statements in interviews and debates—even using Trump's nickname for the senator, "Lyin' Ted."

Now that the O'Rourke campaign had been shaken from the high road, Cruz's people saw their lead grow. But Beto was determined to carry it in for a touchdown.

We know now that Beto did not break into the end-zone. The Democrats didn't score, and they didn't earn another seat in the Senate. But even in the games lost; there are remarkable plays and beauty in reaching the one-yard line. That was what mattered here. What Beto did in the red zone shaped how every politician played the following season.

Beto's charisma brought him tens of thousands of volunteers who phone banked, registered voters, and walked the blocks of their neighborhoods to get people to the ballot box. People felt like part of his movement. Rather than voting for him, they voted with him. Beto continued to defy the laws of conventional campaigning. In the race's final days, he stopped in small towns—hitting multiple locations in a day and focusing on areas where candidates usually didn't bother visiting. This extra care for passed-over communities especially resonated with people of color. Beto came into their shopping mall parking lots and told them that their vote mattered and that their community needed to be represented. He told people that state-wide races had overlooked for decades. These small towns and neighborhoods without consistent voters had been passed over by Democrat and Republican candidates alike, but Beto saw them. Maybe it was because he wasn't a typical politician or because he was the first of a new grassroots breed of politician, but he saw every Texan.

We shouldn't have been surprised by this clear vision. While Beto served in Congress and for the El Paso City Council, he worked closely with the area's richest business moguls, many of whom were staunchly Republican, to get millions in transportation funding. In the words of one of those local moguls, Ted Houghton told *The Texas Tribune*, "We shared a common goal, the goal was to move El Paso in a different direction." Beto did not limit himself to support from the Democratic establishment. He sought the backing of any Texans who could help make his state better. He wanted a better El Paso and would reach across the aisle to do it, and many believed he could do the same for the entire state.

Full transparency: I was caught up in this mayhem. Growing up in a red state with parents from the Northeast, I had never seen an election with so much energy. Aside from the election of Barack Obama, every other race in my life seemed to have had a predetermined outcome. At this point, it did feel like every vote mattered, that this election would be decided not by historical trends or expensive pollsters but by ordinary Texans casting their vote.

Ted Cruz's campaign had eighteen paid staffers. Beto's had 805, according to records obtained by *The Texas Tribune*, not to mention the swarm of volunteers flocking to the O'Rourke camp. It was a moment ripe for a political upset. Cruz pulled out the big guns, and President Trump came to Texas again to rally people behind the man he had called "Lyin' Ted." The irony was not lost on voters. They quickly accepted that enemies became friends when a more significant threat loomed, and Beto had become larger than life.

When the numbers rolled in, 8.3 million Texans had cast their ballot. Fifty-three percent of voters participated in democracy—which according to Kirk Goldsberry was the largest turnout for a midterm election in recent history. Despite visiting every county, Beto pulled the most significant wins from the largest counties. He took Cruz by a two-to-one margin in Dallas County. However, as the rural areas began to report their numbers, the gap closed, and Cruz took the lead. Ted Cruz beat Beto O'Rourke by 2.6 percentage points—which amounts to 222,000 or so votes.

Notice that when you hear about this race, it's never "when Cruz beat Beto." The headlines have always called it Beto's Senate Race. Cruz may have won, but it was Beto's race from the beginning. Maybe the GOP could have squashed Beto from the start. Giving him that early grace because they perceived Beto not to be a threat was a big mistake. I'm sure Cruz's team and long-time GOP leaders hoped Beto would be a flash in the pan—a moment but nothing more. They were wrong.

The early days of the 2020 presidential race, the one with a Democrat field so wide you could drive cattle through it, seem like a lifetime ago. But looking back at the thousands of Texas democrats who were so hopeful during Beto's Senate race, it seemed inevitable that Beto would be put firmly on the national stage once again. He announced his presidential bid in March of 2019. He did it in a video in typical, relaxed Beto fashion, sitting on the couch with his wife. People put tape over the "Senate" on their "Beto for Senate" yard signs and wrote in thick black Sharpie, "PRESIDENT."

In Texas, Beto had the advantage of being the only Democrat in the race. This presidential primary put him up against the leading Democrats from every corner of the country. He didn't last long in this new environment and officially dropped out of the race in November 2019. Was it the *Vanity Fair* piece that portrayed him as the next Kennedy? Did Pete Buttigieg steal his thunder of being the young and locally focused guy? Maybe it was Joaquin Castro also coming into the race from Texas?

It probably had something to do with when he said, "Hell yes, we're going to take your AR-15, your AK-47." That remark was in response to gun violence in his hometown of El Paso, but going after the Second Amendment and might of the NRA while still in a primary proved to be an unwise political move. Even without that one line, it was unlikely Beto would win the primary, let alone the presidency. Vying for the Democratic nomination, he pulled away from the more moderate stance that endeared him to many Texans. It wasn't just the mandatory gun buybacks; *Texas Tribune* reported he also said religious institutions should lose tax-exempt status if they opposed same-sex marriage. Beto started running left and, in doing so, alienated the very supporters who catapulted him to stardom.

Enter "Powered By People." Imagine coming off of back-to-back losses—losing in your home state and then again on the national stage. You'd probably take some time to regroup, lick your wounds, maybe even change careers. Two months after Beto dropped out of the presidential race, he started his own PAC. In an email to his supporters, he wrote that the group would bring "together volunteers from around the state to work on the most important races in Texas." He defined the organization's mission as flipping Texas congressional seats, unseating Republican senator John Cornyn, and getting his state to blue for the presidential race.

Beto was supposed to be the "people, not PACs" guy, and here he was starting his own political action committee. In an interview with *The Texas Tribune* in December 2019, he explained himself to reporters: "There literally was no other legal organization that would allow us to raise money and spend money to help organize people in Texas." Powered By People is, in political jargon, a "hybrid PAC" because it contains two accounts. The first account functions like a traditional PAC and limits individual donations to $5,000 a year. The second works like a super PAC that can take in unlimited amounts of money. Beto's PAC has scruples with self-imposed rules of not taking any funding from corporations or labor organizations.

The fund makes no direct contributions to candidates. Instead, it uses the money for voter outreach like phone banking. All of this sounds as sweet as the yellow rose of Texas. But did Powered by the People achieve any of their goals?

Let's break Powered By People's goals down one at a time, starting with defeating Senator Cornyn.

1. DEFEAT REPUBLICAN SENATOR JOHN CORNYN

Senator Cornyn had a front-row seat to the Beto-Cruz race of 2018, so his team took Democrat challenger MJ Hegar seriously from the beginning. Cornyn hired a campaign manager in January of 2019 and lined up endorsements from President Trump and other big-name Republicans. The four-term senator prepared to throw his weight around. Powered By People swooped to Hegar's side, and Beto told viewers during a fundraising event, "If you want to end not only Donald Trump but Trumpism in America, it is essential we defeat John Cornyn." Over and over, Beto would drive home Cornyn's votes for Trump policies and acquittal in the impeachment trial. Hegar even called Cornyn a "spineless bootlicker," saying Cornyn was a puppet for President Trump. Unfortunately, this made the campaign anti-Cornyn and not pro-Hegar.

Cornyn's approval rating from Republicans was above 65 percent running up to the election and slunk into the single digits among Democrats, according to The Texas Politics Project at the University of Texas at Austin. But no one can win Texas with Democratic votes alone, and even those Democrats needed to be excited about who they were supporting. Hegar didn't have the same magnetism that carried Beto to almost defeating Cruz, and inversely, people didn't hate Cornyn the way they hated Cruz.

Beto's persona and national recognition stole the spotlight from Hegar, and Cornyn's team capitalized on this moment to pin all of Beto's views onto their Democrat challenger. However, Hegar and Beto didn't see eye to eye on an issue that runs deep in the heart of Texas. While Beto was for mandatory buybacks of assault-style guns, Hegar took a centrist stance and believed that this form of confiscation would not be effective. It didn't matter. Hegar was labeled as the woman who also wanted to take your guns. The NRA gave her an F rating and ran ads saying, "Defend freedom, Defeat MJ Hegar." The conflation of the two Democrat characters might have cost Hegar the race. But this didn't mean that Cornyn's team sat comfortably. In an email to donors, Cornyn stated, "Texas' least favorite politician has teamed up with my opponent, Hollywood Hegar, to raise big money from their liberal base. It's a political match made in heaven for coastal elites . . . [let's] make sure Beto doesn't help MJ flip Texas blue." Those are not the words of a politician expecting an easy victory.

Cornyn won by just over nine percentage points on election night, as reported by Politico. A close race in politics would be below the five-point margin, and a comfortable win is in the double digits, so the outcome is competitive but not remarkable. However, since Republicans have held both Texas Senate seats since 1988 and usually win by landslide margins, this was a win for the Democrats. Republicans have held both seats in the Senate since 1988. Hegar proved that Beto's movement had grown roots and would challenge for Republicans in all future elections. Texas Republicans could no longer coast through the election season. They still gripped the state but not with the same iron-clad fist. If a moderate Democrat could escape Beto's shadow or if Beto himself rebranded back to his Senate-race days, Texas would be plucked from the Republicans. I believe if Beto had kept his centrist positions, he could have delivered Hegar a victory or at least closed the gap to under three percentage points.

2. FLIPPING CONGRESSIONAL SEATS

SPECIAL ELECTION TEXAS HOUSE DISTRICT TWENTY-EIGHT

The Texas Tribune reported that Powered By People galvanized 1,100 volunteers to knock on 41,000 doors in the weeks leading up to Democratic candidate Eliz Markowitz's effort to flip District Twenty-Eight in the Texas House of Representatives. She lost by under 13,000 votes, according to Ballotpedia. Republican Gary Gates took Texas House District Twenty-Eight with a winning margin of 16 percentage points. However, 20 percent of registered voters participated in this notably high runoff election. While Powered By People mobilized a significant part of the electorate, backing from Governor Greg Abbott and other Republicans sealed Gates a win.

This district was targeted because the incumbent Republican, Dan Crenshaw, had a narrow victory in 2018. Texas Democrats believed his Houston district was ready for change. However, Crenshaw had grown his reputation while in office. *The Texas Tribune* reported he had $1.6 million to jumpstart his road to reelection. District Two in Harris County is 50 percent minority and skews young and educated, according to DataUSA, making it seem perfect for Democrat candidate Sima Ladjevardian. She was an Iranian immigrant and cancer survivor, running as an advocate for affordable health care in a district where *The Texas Tribune* reported one in seven children lacked health insurance. She was also a firm believer in the Second Amendment and promoted legislation to keep Houston the nation's energy capital. As a former campaign adviser to Beto O'Rourke, she naturally received his endorsement. Nevertheless, Crenshaw shot past her in fundraising and won, taking 55.6 percent of the vote, according to *The New York Times*.

3. THIRTY-EIGHT ELECTORAL VOTES FOR JOE BIDEN

I remember sitting on the couch in my apartment watching the votes come in on election night in 2020. One of the many reporters I was following said something along the lines of "If you're in Texas and excited that it's blue, go ahead and take a picture of your screen because that's going to change eventually as the votes from rural areas come in." I took a picture of the TV screen because it was weird seeing Texas filled in blue. This year was the first vote count I had watched from beginning to end—and that was a very late night. Did anyone really think Texas would flip blue? Yes, many Democrat hopefuls from within the state and across the country. I had friends from each coast messaging me, "Do you see it! Do you see Texas right now!"

It didn't flip, and it probably won't flip in 2024. But after that? Who knows.

Ultimately, Democrats flipped not a single Texas house seat during the 2020 election cycle and failed to deliver the state to Biden. This moment was a massive blow to Powered By People and the Texas Democrats. Everyone on the left was invigorated to potentially make the Texas house blue after twelve seats flipped during the 2018 elections, but they missed the mark. Frankly, Beto and his PAC have a losing record—since they entered the national stage, they haven't brought a candidate victory. However, this is not a total failure.

Political gains are not a bamboo shoot that grows overnight. They are like a Texas Ash, starting as a small sapling but eventually, and with proper care, growing into a sturdy tree that provides shade for the neighborhood. I dare to say the Republican Party understands this better than any other political group—and that is why Powered by the People and the work of Beto O'Rourke will stay on the map. Beto's losses today are the foundations of his gains tomorrow. Texas may technically be a red state, but it's no longer an easy sweep for the Grand Old Party.

Every single Texan knows who Beto is, and now he wields an entire PAC. His wins have been few, but his success in shaping the way Texas votes has been monumental. Beto took grassroots organizing to a new level. He was not deterred by the historical stronghold of the Republican

Party, but instead sought out new voters in every county of the state. His work demonstrated how even the reddest states can be competitive when more people vote. It is indicative of the mixing and flipping of red and blue in America today; if a state like Texas can become a battle-ground, then anywhere can be a place of political change.

CHAPTER 3

MADISON CAWTHORN STEALS HEARTS

Madison Cawthorn is something of a political heartthrob in conservative circles. He's young, conventionally handsome, and has a tragic backstory that could be straight out of a John Green novel. But he is not all flag-waving and baby-kissing. Allow me to introduce the Republican representative from North Carolina's Eleventh District properly.

One of the first things you'll notice about Madison is that he uses a wheelchair. In April 2014, when he was only eighteen, he was in a tragic car accident that left him partially paralyzed from the waist down. Here is the first bump in his story. Cawthorn claimed in a 2017 speech that his friend, who was driving the car at the time, left him "to die in a fiery tomb." However, the friend, Bradley Ledford, claimed he helped rescue Cawthorn from the wreckage. On election night in 2020, Cawthorn introduced Ledford as the man who saved his life, quietly confirming that his original story was a lie. Ledford told *People Magazine* in an interview, "I guess he hasn't made a public statement yet [about the truth of the crash] because he doesn't want to go back on it or prove that he was falsely speaking before? I don't know."

The world of politics does not forgive people who admit their mistakes or change their minds; it's almost better to keep plowing forward and make pointed statements (like a congressman introducing his friend as the man who saved his life) rather than directly issuing a correction.

The tabloids flocked to this drama between two childhood best friends, but a closer look reveals that the false accusations against Ledford are only just the tip of the iceberg for Cawthorn's shrouded past.

A 2020 campaign ad voiceover states that Madison Cawthorn "planned on serving his country in the Navy with a nomination to the US Naval Academy in Annapolis, but all that changed in the spring of 2014 when tragedy struck." However, in a 2017 disposition, Cawthorn stated he was rejected from the Naval Academy before his accident. Cawthorn also claimed he was accepted to Princeton and Harvard but later said some of his statements on college acceptances were "not accurate."

Cawthorn eventually landed at Patrick Henry College in Purcellville, Virginia. The institution has been consistently recognized by the Young America's Foundation as one of the top conservative colleges in the nation. This conservative haven became the setting for his alleged sexual misconduct. Leah Petree and Caitlin Coulter, two students with Cawthorn at the time, have come forward and shared their stories with *The Washington Post*. Petree recalled, "He asked me to go on a fun drive. I had a boyfriend, so I was not going in the car with him. I told him no." However, in October of 2016, Petree had another encounter with Cawthorn, who was harassing another female student. When Petree tried to stick up for the girl Cawthorn called her "just a little, blonde, slutty American girl." She commented, "I remember at the time my eyes stinging with tears." Unfortunately, it is a common scenario for women to be harassed for reacting negatively to a hostile man's advances. He didn't technically break any laws, because federally the only place sexual harassment is explicitly illegal is in the workplace, but his actions still constituted sexual advances that would be considered unlawful in reasonable and public circumstances. A clear pattern of predatory behavior had begun to surface.

Michael Kranish interviewed numerous former students of Cawthorn's university, and many commented that they were warned by residential advisors and classmates not to go on drives with Cawthorn. One girl didn't get the memo. Caitlin Coulter went on one of these "fun drives" with him. Coulter recalled, "There was a specific point in which he grew frustrated, and I shut him down basically—by not responding to some of the advances he was making. And he got upset, and he turned the car around and drove very like, violently is the best way to describe it. Violently back to campus. It was very scary.... It seemed it was very clearly because he was upset I had turned him down or refused his advances."

None of this looks good for Cawthorn, but when asked about the allegations against him on the campaign trail in 2020, he replied, "If I have a daughter, I want her to grow up in a world where people know to explicitly ask before touching her. If I had a son, I want him to be able to grow up in a world where he would not be called a sexual predator for trying to kiss someone." Separate from the context of Cawthorn's story, I believe most reasonable people would agree with him. However, knowing he was the guy who didn't explicitly ask before touching Caitlin Coulter and then was called a sexual predator, it is more challenging to be on his side.

You might be wondering how someone with such a checkered past at the age of twenty-five could successfully enter politics—especially when all of this information is widely and publicly accessible. If you're cynical, you might think politics is the perfect place for this sort of person to absorb the spotlight.

A lot is going on behind that boyish grin, but one thing is definitely true. It is an incredible feat to go from a Naval Academy reject and college dropout suffering from paralysis and running from sexual misconduct allegations to the youngest member in the US House of Representatives.

His political journey began with the Republican primary, where he competed against Lynda Bennett. *The Mountaineer,* a local North Carolina paper, reported Bennett was endorsed by Senator Ted Cruz of Texas and President Donald Trump. She was a state senator, had the proper endorsements, and the most funding out of her competitors. However, she won the March 3, 2020 primary by a shallow margin that forced a runoff. Cawthorn defeated Bennett using a strategy I'll refer to as label application. He put Bennett in a box saying her big-name endorsements were proof she was part of the establishment and would make decisions based on what those endorsers wanted rather than on the needs of the people of her district.

The most significant blow to Bennett's campaign, though, was an unsolicited mass text message sent to nearly everyone in North Carolina's Eleventh Congressional District, obtained by Politico. It held a message that Lynda Bennett was a "Never Trumper," complete with an audio recording of Bennett stating:

I'm never Trump. So now what? What are you going to do? Going to ask me to go out there and help Trump get elected? And you want me to help organize one hundred people to come and work the polls to get Trump elected when I am not for him? I am against him— never Trump!

Bennett claimed that the clip was taken out of context, and later a thirty-seven-minute audio clip of the meeting would prove her right. The meeting was of Haywood County Republicans discussing who they should support in the election and making arguments for not alienating anti-Trump republicans. Listening to the extended version, you hear Bennett say, "You can't be never-Trump, you want me to go out there and organize a hundred people to work the polls to get Trump elected when I am against him. . . . What are you going to do about people like me? . . . I am being facetious." She was trying to get across that it is a slippery slope for Republicans to start dividing over who is for and against Trump and will cause the party significant issues in the future. But even with the full audio released, voters were not convinced.

The Eleventh District was deeply red and had overwhelmingly voted for President Trump, so this audio was damning. Voters didn't care that it would be illogical for Trump to endorse a candidate who was against him. The origin of this smear campaign is officially unknown, but Politico reported it is rumored to have come from strategists on the Cawthorn campaign. When the number that sent the message was called, it was met with an automated response that it was not in service. Financial forensics of the Cawthorn campaign didn't yield any evidence; SMS-texting services could easily be classified as consulting or another obscure part of the public budget.

Cawthorn continued to lob grenades at Bennett, tweeting on June 17, 2020, "Western North Carolina deserves a Representative that is willing to fight for you. My opponent has continually dodged and avoided debate invites from myself and the GOP. What is she afraid of?" That same month in an interview with the *Hendersonville Lightning*, the local newspaper for the district, Cawthorn again called out his opponent for avoiding debates, sharing, "In my mind, if you're not willing to show up and put on display the way you can defend conservatism or be willing to open yourself to tough questioning from constituents then how are you going to be able to represent them in Washington?"

When asked what he would say to Bennett in a debate, Cawthorn remarked, "My question would be, 'why do you value DC politicians' opinions over the constituents in western North Carolina?' She literally said Jim Jordan, Ted Cruz, Mark Meadows—they're all going to be up there holding me accountable if I mess up. They'll say, Lyndsay, get your head on straight. I'm going to be accountable to the people of western North Carolina. That's why I only accept local endorsements."

Ultimately the combination of attacks on Bennett and focusing on local endorsements (according to the *Hendersonville Lightning,* Cawthorn was endorsed by more than forty county commissioners, sheriffs, and school board members) brought him a decisive victory. Cawthorn earned 65.8 percent of the vote (30,444 votes) while Lynda Bennet received a pale 34.2 percent (15,806 votes), according to Ballotpedia. The 31.6 percent margin of victory called attention to Cawthorn, which he handled with expertise not usually seen in a novice politician. His opponent was endorsed by Trump in a district where Trumpism reigned supreme, and he needed to get into Trump's good graces—not because he could lose to the Democrat opposition in November but because he was expecting a second Trump presidency and being "in" with the big man would catapult his political career. Thus, after his primary win, the Cawthorn campaign released a statement that read:

"I want to make something clear; I support our great president. I do not believe this election has been a referendum on the president's influence. The people of western North Carolina are wise and discerning. You observed both candidates and simply made the choice you believe is best for our district. I look forward to fighting alongside our president after I'm elected in November."

Cawthorn also claimed President Trump called him from Air Force One to congratulate him on his congressional win, telling a Politico reporter, "He was talking about how amazing of a victory it was. He defined it as beautiful. You know, just talking about how impressive it was that we were able to overcome just so many large obstacles that we did." Of course, given Cawthorn's history, this could be an exaggeration of facts or an outright lie. However, Trump did eventually publicly acknowledge Cawthorn according to Politico, saying to him at a public speaking event, "You're going to be a real star, a real star of the party."

A Republican congressman winning in a historically red district isn't notable. Even an underdog winning a Republican primary isn't exciting past a few news cycles. An endorsement from Trump came a dime a dozen among Republican politicians. And politicians exaggerating or lying about their past isn't anything new. So why is Madison Cawthorn a vital case study?

First, his age. He's only twenty-five, which means he could serve half a century in the legislative branch and only be seventy-five—three years younger than President

Biden is now. Madison Cawthorn has the potential to shape the Republican Party and US policy for decades to come. He's also pushing a new brand of Republicans. Conventionally, young people are more likely to lean left and vote Democrat. According to an NBC exit poll in 2020, 65 percent of people ages eighteen to twenty-four voted for Biden, 11 percent more than any other age group. Cawthorn is flipping the script and targeting young voters. He wants to revitalize the Republican Party so it is no longer viewed as the party of the old, white, affluent males. In one campaign video, he laid it out clearly: "I'm a millennial. I represent an emerging generation of Americans who are tomorrow's leaders, most of whom think that Republicans don't care about the disenfranchised, the hurting, and those less fortunate. But nothing could be farther from the truth." He's even gone out on a limb to shift the party's position on health care, telling the *Washington Examiner* that his accident helped him understand why some voters flocked to politicians like Alexandria Ocasio-Cortez, who supported big government spending. He goes on to reflect, "I had over three million dollars in medical debt as an eighteen year old. I would like to be the face of the Republican Party when it comes to health care."

Many young Republicans have begun flocking to Cawthorn. While he doesn't have the same large-scale following of what could be considered his left-wing counterpart, the young Alexandria Ocasio-Cortez, he is gaining traction. It is his calculated vulnerability that draws people to him. He shares the softer moments so you feel like his friend, not his constituent. One of the best examples of this is his proposal to his girlfriend, now wife, Cristina.

I've watched the video saga of his proposal on Instagram, and it is undeniably beautiful. You see real human emotion from Madison. The post is from December 2019 with the caption, "It's taken four months of practice to learn to kneel for this girl, but it was all worth it. SHE SAID YES." He shows himself practicing day after day to be able to kneel for the proposal. At points, he punches the ground in frustration or yells in anguish. He has pillows stacked around him for when he falls; it is not pretty. But then you see him kneeling and asking his girlfriend to marry him, and you can't help but feel your heart squeeze in your chest. His face lights up when she says yes, and he exclaims, "Come kiss me!" It is a fairytale moment that makes you forget about his previous lies and misdirection.

Although a microcosm, this instance speaks to young people wanting to see themselves in their politicians and feel connected to their personal lives. In the social media age, this accessibility is easier than ever before. We are like moths to a flame, seeking to see our leaders in vulnerable or ordinary moments. Texans watched Beto's livestream road trips across the state, young Democrats watch AOC's Instagram stories to see what she's working on in committee meetings, and conservatives follow along Cawthorn's journey to the perfect proposal.

Cawthorn's ability to gain the love of many followers despite his lies is astonishing. He's like a dog that pees in the house. You know it's wrong, you don't like it, but when you look into its eyes and think about all the adorable tricks it can do—you can't stay mad for more than one or two news cycles.

No one should be surprised that the guy who peddled lies about a Naval Academy acceptance to seem more qualified would also jump on disinformation to rally his base.

Cawthorn speaks the language of his supporters, tweeting a six-minute video on December 31, 2020, where he stated, "My first act as a member of Congress will be to object the Electoral College certification of the 2020 election." He regurgitated the punch lines being spread on fringe news networks and social media sites that "Voter fraud is common in America. Those who tell you otherwise are lying." He pushed this information despite the fact that President Trump's attorney general, William Barr, stated these allegations were falsehoods. Courts across the country dismissed more than sixty legal challenges filed by the Trump administration. The evidence just didn't exist Now, if you find this tweet, it comes with a message from Twitter underneath: "This claim of election fraud is disputed, and this tweet can't be replied to, retweeted, or liked due to a risk of violence." That violence was none other than the January 6 insurrection.

One thing must be made clear. It does not matter whether you support Cawthorn's ideology. What matters is that people voted him into office. Maybe for his policies, maybe because they didn't like Bennett, maybe because he was charming—they made a choice.

There are so many moments in his campaign where he could have lost. If more people had come out and voted for Lynda Bennett in the first primary, it never would have gone to a runoff. If more voters had been turned off by the allegations and lies brought to light at the beginning of Cawthorn's campaign, his bid would have been dead in the water.

What we should all learn from Madison is that being young, loud, and personable gets votes. Politicians are no longer confined to button-ups and careful calculations. Americans no longer look for the most qualifications or the best record. We want to feel like our representatives are on our team. This cult of personality can be dangerous. It can make us inclined to let things like sexual assault allegations and bald-faced lies slide. We shouldn't run into the arms of men like Cawthorn without holding them accountable for their mistakes. Instead, we must recognize this Cawthorn variety of politician in our districts and ask ourselves three questions:

- Will they fight for me?
- Will they succeed?
- Will their shortcomings harm my community?

Madison Cawthorn fights every day for the conservatives of NC-11. His weekly newsletters update what he's doing in Washington and his district offices. If you call his offices, they answer on the first ring. He is dedicated.

Madison's successful legislation is no laundry list; he is very new in his role. However, he co-sponsored HR

1276—the Strengthening and Amplifying Vaccination Efforts to Locally Immunize All Veterans and Every Spouse Act, also referred to as the SAVE LIVES Act—which became law in March 2021. Considering he ran on being the face of health care for the Republican Party and a dedication to serving the armed forces, his co-sponsorship of this bill demonstrates he means business.

It remains to be seen if Madison's shortcomings will harm his community. That is why constituents have to stay vigilant and vote with intention.

Cawthorn is a welcome maverick for the GOP, and he is anything but subtle. His most infamous words to date embody his rise to stardom: "I will put the Republican establishment on my shoulders and drag them kicking and screaming back to the Constitution." And the crowd goes wild. If Cawthorn can keep stealing hearts and winning votes, he could be unstoppable.

CHAPTER 4

JUSTICE DEMOCRATS CREATE THE SQUAD

Alexandria Ocasio-Cortez, known widely as "AOC," didn't come to represent New York's Fourteenth Congressional District by chance. It was all part of a very calculated scheme that put four women in House seats in 2018. The mastermind: an organization called Justice Democrats.

According to their website, the group believes "We need a Democratic Party that fights for its voters, not corporate donors, and a new generation of leaders who will fight for our communities and a bold agenda." Their mission, to "elect a mission-driven caucus that will fight for bold, progressive solutions to match the scope and scale of our current crises: skyrocketing inequality, a climate catastrophe, deepening systemic racism, and a corporate takeover of our democracy."

How they accomplish this mission is to put regular people in office. They find potential candidates through nominations. On the website is a pink button that reads, "Nominate a candidate." If you click it, it takes you to a form to fill out some information on the nominee and why you think they should represent their community in government. AOC's brother nominated her—an action whose domino effect shifted the political game.

Today this group of ordinary people-turned-politicians is known as the Squad and includes AOC, Ayanna Pressley, Ilhan Omar, Rashida Tlaib, Jamaal Bowman, Cori Bush, and Marie Newman.

The key to this movement is not flipping districts but rather defeating Democrat incumbents. The four women who won House seats in 2018 and started The Squad all unseated long-time Democrats. AOC did it with a splash.

ALEXANDRA OCASIO-CORTEZ

In New York's Fourteenth District, Representative Joseph Crowley found himself with a primary challenger, which hadn't happened since 2004. His campaign was not concerned with a twenty-eight-year-old political novice. Many believed he would take Pelosi's seat as Speaker of the House. AOC took him out at the knees, winning 57 percent of the vote according to the New York Times.

AOC's race reflects a growing preference within the Democratic Party for leaders who better reflect the demographics of the communities they represent. The Fourteenth District includes the Bronx and Queens, home to a majority of people of color. They had been represented by a middle-aged white man, Joseph Crowley, who lived in northern Virginia. Nothing says out of touch quite like having your permanent residence in an entirely different state than your constituents.

Crowley focused his campaign ads on opposition to President Trump. At the same time, AOC used social media to discuss her support for gun control, the Affordable Care Act, increasing community programs near schools, and the Green New Deal. These issues were pertinent to the lives of the people in her district. They experienced gang-related gun violence and wanted safer streets. According to statistics from Data USA, almost 40 percent relied on government health-care programs and after-school care.

Crowley looked at the forest while AOC saw the trees. Crowley's anti-Trump rhetoric wasn't tangible; it didn't promise anything, and when media pressed him on particular policy issues, he watered-down versions of what AOC already said. AOC would say "abolish ICE"; Crowley would say "reform immigration." AOC said, "Medicare for all"; Crowley said, "expand the Affordable Care Act." AOC was further left and closer to the people he sought to represent.

In 2020 the Fourteenth District of New York elected AOC to a second term, defeating her Republican challenger by nearly 37 percentage points, according to NYT reporting. District Fourteen is hers for now. Justice Democrats made a woman like AOC in Congress possible, and now she is on a quest for sweeping change.

Sweeping change is the crucial difference between The Squad and other Democrats. The days of Nancy Pelosi and Hillary Clinton were rooted in incremental change, one step at a time. The focus was on calculating who held the majority in the bicameral legislature, which bills could get passed, and how to appease the opposite side so that they could make small changes. Justice Democrats and their Squad do not mold to this mentality. They continually propose large-scale changes that fire up their constituents and scare the Republican opposition. In a world where attention is a fleeting commodity, small moves just don't cut it, especially among younger voting blocs. AOC didn't just come to power because she had the proper funding and endorsements; she earned her seat by capturing the people's attention. Ayanna Pressley, Ilhan Omar, and Rashida Tlaib, the other three winning 2018 representatives from Justice Democrats, did the same thing.

AYANNA PRESSLEY

She represents Massachusetts' Seventh District and is its first black congresswoman. Like AOC, she beat a Democrat incumbent in the primary to take her seat at the table. Pressley defeated ten-term incumbent Michael Capuano 58.6 percent to 41.4 percent. While AOC could hold Crowley to the fire for being out of touch with his district, Capuano was deeply embedded in the Massachusetts Seventh. He was the mayor of Somerville for almost a decade before running for the House. While in Congress, he was a member of the Congressional Progressive Caucus. Capuano and Pressley shared many of the same progressive political views. Pressley even stated during a debate, "We will vote the same way, but I will lead differently." The difference that Pressley's campaign pushed was that she lived the experience of being a person of color in America.

In contrast, Capuano, a white man over sixty-five years old, could not share the same empathy. Pressley ran her campaign with a multicultural focus, running TV ads featuring local activists on Telemundo and Univision and placing ads on Hispanic, Haitian, and Chinese media outlets. She went to where her potential voters were instead of focusing on the portion of the electorate that consistently voted. This strategy paid off in dividends; constituents cast 102,067 votes in her primary. In the 2006 primary of Capuano versus Governor Deval Patrick, only 85,051 votes were cast, according to Massachusetts Elections Division records. Expanding the electorate won Pressley the election.

ILHAN OMAR

She was elected in 2018 to represent the Fifth District of Minnesota. She's a refugee who fled with her family from Somalia and eventually settled in Minneapolis, one of the largest Somalian diaspora communities. She was elected to the Minnesota State House in 2016, where she received fifteen seconds of national fame as the first Somali American lawmaker in the US. Omar ran against an incumbent who had held the seat for over four decades in a state district that *The Washington Post* reported was 60 percent white. She won the primary mainly because she could mobilize young people who didn't usually vote and because of her visibility at Black Lives Matter protests throughout the city in 2015. She symbolized the Somali community in Minnesota; her status as a refugee and progressive politician made her an anti-Trump icon. Despite President Trump calling her "an America-hating socialist" at a rally in Minnesota, Omar set her sights higher and ran for Congress.

The Minnesota Fifth had been Keith Ellison's district since 2007, but he was tapped to become the state's attorney general ahead of the 2018 election, leaving the field open. Omar faced a crowded primary field with five other candidates but won 48.2 percent of the vote according to Ballotpedia. She was the first person to wear a hijab on the House floor.

Her next challenge came in 2020, when she was primaried again. This time she had national recognition on her side. She was endorsed by Bernie Sanders, Elizabeth Warren, and Speaker Nancy Pelosi. The Minnesota Fifth is a historically blue district, making the primary the critical race. Now Omar was up against Antone Melton-Meaux, a first-time political candidate.

Melton-Meaux heavily criticized Omar, telling the *Minnesota Post*, "I was hopeful that she would use her platform to do great work for the district. But what I've seen since then is someone that doesn't show up for votes and someone that doesn't show up for voters." According to GovTrack, Omar missed 5.7 percent of votes in 2019, tying with five other representatives for fifty-fifth most absent. While missing votes is not a good way to win over voters, this revelation didn't impact her campaign's momentum. To the naked eye, the policies the two candidates supported were virtually the same, except when it came to Israel. Omar has consistently spoken out in support of the Palestinian people, whereas Melton-Meaux was vehemently pro-Israel. Both candidates raised over four million dollars and were heavily funded by out-of-state donors. NPR reported 91 percent of Omar's funds came from out of the state compared to 85 percent of Melton-Meaux's. The massive share of non-Minnesota donations demonstrates how important this race was to factions within the Democratic Party and pro-Israel groups. Melton-Meaux gained support from Iris and Shalom Maidenbaum, Howard Jonas, and other large donors to Trump and Ted Cruz. Republican influence in a Democrat primary proves how formidable Omar had become in her first term and that they feared her gaining more political traction. Ultimately, Omar prevailed with 58.2 percent of the vote compared to Melton-Meaux's 38.5 percent according to NPR.

RASHIDA TLAIB

She was elected to represent Michigan's Thirteenth in 2018. The opportunity came when Representative John Conyers Jr. resigned over sexual harassment allegations. Conyers Jr. had held his seat for fifty-two years, making this moment a unique opening for change for the district. No Republican was on the ticket for the 2018 race, making the primary the sole decider of who would represent the Thirteenth. Tlaib ran against Detroit City Council President Brenda Jones. Both women focused on equity in education, closing corporate tax loopholes, and reducing recidivism and mass incarceration during their campaigns. Due to Conyers Jr. vacating his seat, there was a primary to determine who would finish his term and another to decide who would be sworn in for the new term. Even more confusing is that Jones won the primary to complete the term, and Tlaib won the primary for the new term.

Tlaib won by only 900 votes. She joined the Squad but without the winning margins of the other members of the group. Brenda Jones lost but filed to run against Tlaib in the 2020 election. The field was different now that Tlaib had recognition in her district. The congresswoman had gone viral for comments made during a reception after she was sworn into office in January of 2019: "Don't you ever, ever let anybody take away your roots, your culture, who you are. Ever. Because when you [hang on to those things], people love you, and you win. And when your son looks at you and says, 'Mama, look. You won.' Bullies don't win. And I said, 'Baby; they don't because we're gonna go in there and we're gonna impeach that motherfucker.'" This behavior would have been frowned upon in a different time and place, but her rhetoric energized her district. She was before them, uncensored and fully human. Again and again, she showed this very human and emotive side which resonated with her voters. They liked her because she acted as a reflection of them rather than a member of the political elite. Her authenticity shined through in 2020 when she defeated Jones in the primary by 32 percent of the vote.

SQUAD UP

Dismantling the Democratic establishment is an immense undertaking. The reason the Justice Democrats have been so successful is that they build from within. The organization understands that it is better to develop new talent to champion their progressive ideals than to persuade the existing politicians to accept their ideology. They build from the ground up, which means if people actively participate in local elections, they can elect new officials who will put their concerns on the state and even the national agenda.

The stories of Tlaib, Pressley, Omar, and Ocasio-Cortez serve as an important reminder. Just because the politician is from the same political party as you doesn't mean they represent your needs. In a two-party system, there is a wide variety of ideas that fall under Democrat or Republican. Do you want a Crowley or an AOC? You decide when you vote in your primaries.

Justice Democrats have put ten people in Congress (the other six being Jamaal Bowman, NY-16; Pramila Jayapal, WA-07; Cori Bush, MO-01; Marie Newman, IL-03; Ro Khanna, CA-17; and Raul Grijalva, AZ-03). They are already setting up candidates for the 2022 primaries in TN-05, OH-11, and NY-12.

CHAPTER 5

YOUNG REPUBLICANS NATIONAL FEDERATION

While the Justice Democrats were founded in early 2017, the Young Republicans National Federation (YRNF) dates back to 1931. The YRNF is the oldest political youth organization in the United States and serves as the methodical counterpart to the Justice Democrat's spunky campaigns. In essence, the two organizations have the same goal: provide grassroots support to candidates and engage young voters. According to their website, "In 2020, the Young Republicans National Federation deployed volunteers into twenty-five states over ten weeks during the fall campaign with Young Republicans, making more than twenty-three million voter contacts, sending twenty-four Young Republicans to Congress and thousands of Young Republicans to state legislatures." They also have a state federation in all fifty states to organize locally.

They even have their own group of politically famous candidates, though none have gained the same level of social media prowess as the Squad. Their trophies are

Madison Cawthorn (NC-11), Matt Gaetz (FL-1), Senator Josh Hawley (MO), and Lauren Boebert (CO-3).

MATT GAETZ FL-1

Gaetz was first elected in 2016. Initially, he vied for the state Senate seat his father had just vacated due to term limits. He would have faced off against Bay County Commissioner George Gainer in a race expected to be one of the most expensive in the state. Realizing this intense competition, Gaetz switched gears and decided to throw his name in for the First District of Florida. Republican representative Jeff Miller retired from Congress, leaving the seat vacant. Just like members of the Squad, Gaetz did not flip districts. He pursued power in an already red district. Unlike the Justice Democrats, he was not a political newcomer. His father was entrenched in Florida politics, and he grew up in the political sphere.

While the Squad relied on small individual donations, endorsements from the National Rifle Association, Florida Right to Life, Humane Society Legislative Fund, and other interest groups carried Gaetz to victory over his primary opponents. He won his seat again in 2018, with much more ease. The community recognized him and he had gained some celebrity from being acknowledged by President Trump. Once it became clear he had won the 2018 primary, he proclaimed, "Our community embraces the conservative values that make America great, whether it is rebuilding our military, securing our borders, defending the Second Amendment, or protecting the sanctity of life. I look forward to working with northwest Florida residents, local businesses, and President Trump to continue improving our tremendous community."

Gaetz emphasized the issues that regular people in northwest Florida deeply cared about resolving. While he supported keeping the corporate tax rate and taxes on the wealthy low, when Matt spoke to the crowds, he zeroed in on their pro-life, pro-defense, and anti-immigration values. He was further right than his colleagues, and his constituents championed him for it. Matt sought to defund Planned Parenthood and co-sponsored HR816/S2464, a bill to implement equal protection under the Fourteenth Amendment for the right to life of each pre-born human person. When it comes to defense, his posture was hawkish. He supported American intervention in the Middle East beyond air support and sought to defeat militant Islam abroad. He "opposed any form of amnesty, fought cash welfare payments for illegal immigrants, and voted against offering them in-state college tuition, even when other Republicans supported it," according to OnTheIssues. Just as AOC pulls the Democrats left, Gaetz tugs the Republicans right.

His website highlights his accomplishments: "During his first term in Congress, Matt helped pass the landmark Tax Cuts and Jobs Act, which provided a much-deserved tax cut to millions of American families and businesses. Matt is also leading the fight to expose corruption in the FBI, the Justice Department, and the Clinton Foundation, regularly appearing on cable news to bring accountability to our government and defend the Trump administration."

Many of his constituents are skeptical of government, and the Gaetz team is keen to speak to those concerns. He built an image as a good man; described by his campaign team, he "is a member of the First Baptist Church of Fort Walton Beach. He has one son, Nestor, and Matt has described raising him as the most rewarding thing I've done in my life."

A politician who's a good Christian with nicknames like "the Trumpiest Congressman" is what the Florida First wanted. Thus, anything contrary to this good man image could be particularly damaging. Gaetz risked a fall from grace when allegations of his illegal drug use and sexual misconduct came to light. Luckily these allegations came to light after he had been elected to a third term. However, the case gained traction, and in April 2021, the House Ethics Committee launched an investigation. To be clear, an investigation does not necessarily mean guilt, but American voters can quickly lose trust and turn on their political leaders.

SENATOR JOSH HAWLEY OF MISSOURI

Unlike the other candidates we've discussed, Hawley flipped his seat by beating an incumbent of the other party, in his case, Democrat Claire McCaskill. He was the youngest member of the US Senate during the 116th Congress. Similar to his YRNF colleagues, Hawley entered Congress as a political insider. He was attorney general of Missouri from 2017 to 2019 and had prior clerkships at the US Court of Appeals Tenth Circuit and the United States Supreme Court.

Hawley won 51.4 percent of the vote in 2018, achieving victory over McCaskill, who had 45.6 percent. The race was crucial in determining which party would hold control of the Senate and consequently gained national interest. President Trump visited Missouri on multiple occasions to help boost Hawley. Trump even told voters during a September 2018 rally in Springfield, Missouri, to vote for Hawley "because you're voting for me [Trump]," as reported by *The Kansas City Star*. Trump carried Missouri in 2016. Therefore, by driving the message that Trump supporters should also vote for Hawley, they created significant momentum around the future senator.

Like Matt Gaetz, Hawley has on occasion landed himself in hot water. Following the January 6 insurrection support for him in Missouri plummeted. He was seen as partially responsible for the storming of the Capitol because he didn't vote to certify the 2020 election results and that he fanned the flames of conspiracy. In a matter of hours, Hawley was dropped from a book deal with Simon & Schuster, which issued a statement proclaiming, "As a publisher, it has always been our mission to amplify a variety of voices and viewpoints; at the same time, we take seriously our larger public responsibility as citizens, and cannot support Senator Hawley after his role in what became a dangerous threat to our democracy and freedom."

Hawley's biggest donor, the CEO of Tamko Building Products, David Humphreys, called on the US Senate to censure Hawley for provoking the capital riots and said the senator was "an anti-democracy populist." Former

Senator John Danforth went so far as to tell the *St. Louis Post-Dispatch* that supporting Hawley was "the worst mistake I ever made in my life." It only got worse for the Missouri senator as calls for him to resign started. The Mizzou Law Student Bar Association released a statement: "Senator John Hawley, once Professor Hawley in the classrooms of Hulston Hall, has violated the oath he swore upon his election to the United States Senate. Our Student Bar Association encourages him to resign for the sake of our state, the benefit of our country, but most importantly, for the protection of the rule of law." The editorial boards of *The Kansas City Star* and *the St. Louis Post-Dispatch* both called for his resignation. Luckily for Hawley, he won't be up for re-election for a few more years and thus has time to bring his constituents back on his side.

LAUREN BOEBERT CO-3

While Gaetz and Hawley were political insiders, Boebert was a newcomer. She owns a restaurant called Shooters Grill in Rifle, Colorado. It lives up to the name: Waitresses open carry while on shift. You may have heard of Boebert as the woman who promised to carry a gun to Congress. Of course, she was stopped by Capitol police; no firearms are allowed on the House floor. But her rise to Republican stardom is very similar to the path of AOC. Both women ran primaries against incumbents; neither had prior political experience and represented some of the extreme values of their political parties. Frankly, Boebert would hate such a comparison. She is the antithesis of AOC in terms of policy.

In an interview on local television shortly after she announced her candidacy, Next 9NEWS journalist Kyle Clark remarked, "Your campaign announcement didn't mention Congressman Tipton [the four-term incumbent] by name, but it did spend quite a bit of time talking about Democratic Congresswoman Alexandria Ocasio-Cortez of New York. Are you running against her or Tipton?" Boebert replies, "I'm absolutely running against her. . . . I am ready to be the one that steps up for conservative values and takes on AOC."

At first glance, it seems like a bizarre strategy to initiate a district-wide campaign by announcing you're going to take down a representative on the other side of the country. Still, the constituents in this district saw the ideology and policies put forth by progressives like AOC as extremely concerning. Boebert's message was that she was going to fight against the left and stick to conservative values. She went on to tell reporter Clark, "I think our congressman [Tipton] forgot who he was a little bit. I looked him up, and there was some questionable votes . . . in reference to Planned Parenthood funding. Abortions are just not conservative values. I believe that my constituents will sleep well at night knowing that I will check off every conservative checkbox that there is, and I want them to hold me accountable to that." This rhetoric played well for Boebert, and she received 55 percent of the vote compared to Tipton's 45 percent in the primary, according to Ballotpedia. She went on to win the general and is a freshman Congress member alongside Madison Cawthorn.

REPUBLICAN

YRNF's other successful candidates include Kat Cammack, FL-3; Dan Crenshaw, TX-2; Byron Donalds, FL-19; Mike Gallagher, WI-8; Anthony Gonzales, OH-16; Tony Gonzales, TX-23; Lance Gooden, TX-5; Ashley Hinson, IA-1; Trey Hollingsworth, IN-9; Nicole Malliotakis, NY-11; Brian Mast, FL-18; Peter Meijer, MI-3; Guy Reschenthaler, PA-14; Jason Smith, MO-8; Elise Stefanik, NY-21; Bryan Steil, WI-1; William Timmons, SC-4; and Lee Zeldin, NY-1.

What does this mean for future elections?

We will keep seeing younger and newer faces on both sides of the aisle. These new politicians will continue to change the fabric of politics as we know it. Gone are the days when the right pedigree and endorsements guaranteed a primary victory. Instead politicians must connect with the root values of their future constituents and convey a warrior-like desire to fight for them in Washington.

The energy younger generations of political leaders bring to the ballot box necessitates that the old establishment update their tactics or risk being left behind. It is exciting to see new people take the lead, but we must also recognize that part of their appeal is derived from their extreme positions. These politicians beat more moderate candidates and launched to a level of stardom because of their far-left or far-right policies.

There are almost no moderates among this new cohort of politicians, which means that in comfortably red and blue areas the primary election will be the most critical.

If it is understood that in a red state whoever wins the primary will also win the general, the primary election is where constituents select their next leader. Whether you are on board with these more extreme positions or desire a moderate political outlook, you must make that known by voting in the primary.

From what the YRNF and Justice Democrats have demonstrated with their successful candidates, we know that for many future races the ideological battle will happen during the primary.

CHAPTER 6

STACEY ABRAMS FLIPS GEORGIA

Donald Trump and Stacey Abrams have at least two things in common.

They both refused to concede once they lost their elections. Now Abrams has said comparing the two is "simply different . . . apples and bowling balls," but to my Republican friends in the South, they're both round. When our forty-fifth president refused to concede, it was because he genuinely believed or wanted his supporters to think he had won the 2020 election. The *Financial Times* reported Abrams refused to concede because "there were a series of actions taken that impeded the ability of voters to cast their ballots, and in almost every one of those circumstances, the courts agreed, as did the state legislature." The other thing Trump and Abrams share is wielding a large amount of political power even when not holding a seat in government. Donald Trump continues to pull strings in the Republican Party, and Abrams did more than anyone else to flip Georgia from red to blue in 2020.

Stacey Abrams is the main reason the Democrats were able to win Georgia in 2020 and gain two Senate seats. Her work registering voters and encouraging people to turn out for the election helped Biden win Georgia by a count of ten thousand votes according to Reuters. She didn't stop in November but kept pushing underserved communities to participate in the January runoff that gave the state two Democratic senators. In an April 2021 speech in Duluth, Georgia, President Biden spoke of Abrams saying she "could be anything she wants to be, from whatever she chooses to president" and went on to thank her for "empowering people to vote and make their voices heard."

STACEY ABRAMS

Abrams came to the political scene in 2006 when she ran for the Georgia state legislature and became the first woman to lead either party in the Georgia General Assembly. While she stands for liberal values, her focus has been on expanding voting access in Georgia. This pursuit was sparked, in part, by the Supreme Court's 2013 ruling that removed one of the provisions of the Voting Rights Act of 1965. The provision had forced nine states with a history of racism to obtain federal approval of any change to their election laws. Retracting this provision meant Alabama, Alaska, Arizona, Georgia, Louisiana, Mississippi, South Carolina, Texas, and Virginia could make up their election laws without oversight. Voting law changes started popping up in all nine of these states. In reaction, Abrams co-founded the New Georgia Project in 2014, a nonpartisan effort to register and civically engage

Georgians. NGP has been extraordinarily successful and, as of 2019, had registered almost half a million Georgians in all 159 of Georgia's counties. Their success is due to their registration model, where they go to the people instead of asking people to come to them. They walk neighborhoods, college campuses, and even churches—all to make it easy for people to become registered voters. Co-founding an organization that registered half a million people in your state is a massive accomplishment, but that was only the beginning for Abrams.

In 2018, she decided to run for governor of Georgia. The first hurdle was the Democratic primary, where she faced off against Stacey Evans. Asma Khalid, a reporter from NPR, put it simply "the two candidates running for governor in the Georgia Democratic primary on May 22 have plenty of similarities: They're both women named Stacey; they're both former legislators in the Georgia House of Representatives; they're both lawyers; and they're both calling for similar progressive politics, such as expanding Medicaid." Abrams focused her campaign energy on persuading communities of color, believing that engaging minority voters could push her to victory. Meanwhile, Evans thought victory would come from rural areas and bringing moderate Republicans to her side.

Yes, one black Stacey and one white Stacey were running to be the Democratic contender for the governorship, but that didn't define their supporters. To say that this primary was divided along racial lines would be an unjust oversimplification. However, many Georgians recognized the gravity of what a black woman running for governor in the general election would look like, given the state's deep racial tensions. This was one of Evans's main advantages. One of her African American supporters, Lisa Cunningham, even predicted that "an African American person of her stature cannot today win in the state of Georgia in the general election." Despite this sentiment, Stacey Abrams won the Democratic primary with 76.5 percent of the vote. Evans immediately backed Abrams, saying Democrats must "find a unified voice to rally against Trump." Now it was time for the real fun to begin—the general election.

It's no secret that Stacey Abrams lost the general election to Brian Kemp, but how she lost would raise more questions than answers. Georgia's voting procedure sends voters who have not cast a ballot in three years a notice asking them to confirm their residence; if they don't respond to the notice, they are marked as inactive. They are removed from the voter rolls if they don't vote in two more general elections after receiving inactive status, meaning they are no longer registered to vote. According to *The Guardian*, 534,000 voters were removed from the rolls using this method in 2016 and 2017.

There was one wrinkle; 334,134 of those removed from the rolls still lived at the address where they were initially registered. Maybe there should be a better way to contact infrequent voters so a state doesn't have 300,000 voters purged from the rolls because they didn't confirm their address. The political left saw it differently. Their argument was rooted in the idea that Brian Kemp, who was Secretary of State for Georgia during this race, used his power to suppress the vote.

The more alarming statistic is that, according to AP News, 53,000 voter registration applications were on hold, sitting in Brian Kemp's office. As Georgia's Secretary of State, he was in charge of elections and voter registration for the state. That was a massive conflict of interest. According to an analysis from the Associated Press, 70 percent of people on this list were black. Many were not made aware that their registration had been held up. These statistics did not look good for Kemp. Thousands of people had tried to register to vote, but their applications were being held up by his office in a race he ran in, where his opponent was black and the majority of held-up applications were of black constituents. The applications were held up under the pretense that they did not precisely match the information on file with the Georgia Department of Driver Services or the Social Security Administration. This meant a misplaced hyphen or comma would put a hold on your application.

PURGE, PUT ON HOLD, PROTECT THE VOTE?
Marsha Appling-Nunez is one of the Georgia voters whose registration was put on hold. She was never notified of the issue. Instead, she found out while she was showing her college students how to check their voter registration online. She entered her information, and the site revealed she was not registered. Marsha told AP News in 2018, "I was kind of shocked. I've always voted, I try not to miss any elections, even local ones." It is alarming that

Georgians were so swiftly ejected from voter registration, but even more worrisome that they were not notified of this change. If Marsha hadn't checked her enrollment, she wouldn't have known there was an issue until it was too late.

The Kemp administration can argue until their last breath that their regulations were about election security, not voter suppression. However, if the goal is for all Georgians to vote, the system would have a mechanism to notify people who have been removed from the registration list. Imagine your car didn't have a check engine light; how would you know there was an issue? You wouldn't. Sure, you could bring it into the shop every week to double check, but that's an illogical use of time. If you're removed from the voter rolls, you should at minimum have a check engine light and be notified so you can rectify the issue prior to voting.

PROTECT THE VOTE!

Depending on your political affiliation and what information you have already consumed about Georgia, you may feel strongly about the alleged voter suppression. The Heritage Foundation, a conservative think tank in DC, has an election fraud database that tracks proven instances of voter deceit. They have tracked 1,333 cases of election fraud, twenty of which occurred in Georgia. If you think about the seven million voters in Georgia and the number of elections they have voted in over the years, twenty instances of fraud is a remarkably low number. That's less than 0.000003 percent fraud per election.

Since it is not a rampant problem, it should be a no-brainer to notify people if their registration is held up or removed from the voter rolls.

Truthfully, some Republicans will never admit Georgia's procedures are voter suppression, and many Democrats will continue to push the narrative that difficulties in voting are racially charged. We must fix the system that allows for arguments that there's a trade-off between voting access and election security. We can make it easier to vote without jeopardizing the security of the ballot box.

Several lawsuits were filed as a result of this election, and they brought no tangible gains for the people of Georgia. What would have been more helpful was if they updated the voting laws so that people are more effectively notified of their status and have ample time to correct potential mistakes to stay on the voting rolls. If the system truly works, it oppresses no one.

Stacey Abrams lost the governorship because many of her supporters were unable to vote. She would not make the same mistake twice. It became clear that merely registering voters wasn't enough; she had to make sure those applications went through and those people turned out on election day.

In 2020, Abrams was not the candidate. Instead, she campaigned for the Democratic contenders for Georgia's two Senate seats. Enter the next four characters: Democrats

Jon Ossoff and Raphael Warnock, and Republicans David Perdue and Kelly Loeffler.

PERDUE VERSUS OSSOFF

David Perdue served as a Republican senator for Georgia from 2015 to 2021. He was a businessman by trade and held executive positions at Sara Lee, Dollar General, and Reebok. He became known for his conservative views and even sought to ban same-sex marriage.

Jon Ossoff would take Perdue's Senate seat. Also a businessman, he has served as the CEO of the media company Insight TWI since 2013. He had a failed congressional run in Georgia's Sixth District in 2017. He's in his early thirties, Jewish, supports Israel's security as a homeland for the Jewish people, and is a progressive Democrat.

LOEFFLER VERSUS WARNOCK

Kelly Loeffler was appointed to fill the Senate seat of John Isakson, who retired at the end of 2018. She's a Trump supporter and former Fortune 500 executive, owns a stake in a WNBA team, and is married to Jeffrey Sprecher (the founder and CEO of ICE).

Raphael Warnock, who defeated Loeffler in 2020, is the senior pastor of Ebenezer Baptist Church, a consistent fighter for fair pay and voting rights, and became the eleventh black senator in US history.

The two senatorial elections were in lockstep. Both had strong candidates who hailed from opposite sides of the political spectrum, and all eyes were on Georgia as the results could change which party held power in the Senate.

Ossoff and Warnock were able to win because of on-the-ground organizing and voter mobilization—especially among communities of color. This would not have been possible without Stacey Abrams's groundwork, like the New Georgia Project.

GEORGIA'S UNKNOWN FUTURE

Abrams' wins brought her praise and national attention, but her challengers were not deterred. In March of 2021 Governor Brain Kemp signed Senate Bill 202, which according to Georgia Public Broadcasting is a "ninety-eight-page bill [that] makes dramatic alterations to Georgia's absentee voting rules, adding new identification requirements, moving back the request deadline and other changes after a record 1.3 million absentee ballots overwhelmed local elections officials and raised Republican skepticism of a voting method they created." Some provisions of the bill are positive for voters, like requiring precincts with more than 2,000 voters with voting lines longer than an hour three times during the day to add more voting machines. However, it is clear the bill is centered on decreasing access to absentee voting, the type of voting that Abrams wielded to secure her Democratic victories.

The 2022 midterms and beyond will demonstrate the efficacy of Senate Bill 202 just as much as they will give Abrams an opportunity to demonstrate that her effort to expand the electorate was not temporary. Abrams and the New Georgia Project can knock on doors until their knuckles bleed and Governor Kemp can pass voting bills until he's blue in the face, but what will determine the outcome in Georgia is Georgians themselves. If they get out and vote, despite the limitations, and choose leaders who value high election participation, people like Brian Kemp will lose power. If more people on the other side of the issue vote in higher numbers, people like Brian Kemp will stay in charge.

Many would say Stacey Abrams saved Georgia and saved the Democrats, but the lesson here is not just the power of one woman to change the trajectory of democracy, but rather that one woman cannot protect it alone. The battle for Georgia is far from over.

CHAPTER 7

2020 CENSUS RESULTS AND SHIFTING ELECTORATE

When was the first time the US Census counted your existence?

If you were born in 1991, it would be nine years before the decennial Census came around. If these 1991 babies went to kindergarten at age five in 1996, by 1999, they would have been in the third grade, which means third graders and younger weren't yet included in the census count.

The average class size for primary schools in Texas is 18.9 students, and the average number of students per elementary school in the state is 551, according to the National Center for Education Statistics. Jumble the numbers, and you end up with thousands—even tens of thousands—of kids who wait years to be counted in the Census.

It doesn't seem like a big deal until you realize that states can lose or gain congressional seats based on the flux of their population. In the 2020 Census New York lost a seat by eighty-nine people, and Minnesota held on to one by twenty-six people. That's just a few classrooms. If eighty-nine kids had been born earlier, New York would have kept that seat. And if twenty-six kids had been born later, Minnesota would have lost theirs.

It is important to note that a hundred kids being born earlier or later isn't the only thing that affects Census outcomes. In fact, the Census count can have a high margin of error. One enumerator told me that during the 2020 Census cycle, "hundreds of census takers were encouraged to flub numbers if residents refused to answer properly. While I can't legally release any data I received during my time as an enumerator, I can relay that several people in my district were encouraged to, and several did, falsify their numbers. Some were caught and repri-manded/released from duty; some weren't."

The highlights of any Census are always which states gain or lose congressional districts, and 2020 was no dif-ferent. California, Michigan, Illinois, Ohio, West Virginia, Pennsylvania, and New York all lost one seat, while Ore-gon, Montana, Florida, and North Carolina each gained one seat. Naturally, my home state of Texas had to go big, and we gained two seats.

There are a few commonalities I hear when talking about the Census. For starters, it's not a sexy topic, and I would not advise bringing it up on a date. Typical discourse on the sensual Census is usually limited to the following: "Will there be a citizenship question?"; insert theory about the government using this to track you (yes, some-one actually said this to me while holding an iPhone); a sticky question about gerrymandering; and the classic "Do I actually need to fill that out?" Let's break it down and cut through the partisan fat to get to the real meat of this almighty survey.

THE CITIZENSHIP QUESTION

Are you a United States citizen? Yes or no? Chances are, you are pro-citizenship question if you're anti-immigra-tion and vice versa. I'm not going to tell you a citizenship question is xenophobic or a lack thereof is anti-American. Instead, I'll share why we either need more immigration or for current Americans to start acting like baby boom-ers and churn out kids.

The 2020 Census shows that the US population grew at its slowest pace since the 1930s. The 1930 census showed a 16.2 percent population growth that fell to 7.3 in 1940 but rebounded to 14.5 percent in 1950 and sailed to 18.5 percent in 1960. The decrease in the 1930s was an anomaly due to the Great Depression. However, this time around, the 2020 decrease is not an exception to the rule.

Since the 2000 census, US population growth has been on a decline. The birth rate has hit its lowest in thir-ty-two years, sitting at 1.73 births per mother in January 2020, as reported by Business Insider. Our birth rate is below the replacement rate, meaning that if this trend holds, our population will continue to decline without an outside influx of people (a.k.a. immigrants). Therefore, if we increase immigration, we can reverse the decline and even create population growth. States and communities that accept and attract more immigrants will not just see the economic gains of a population influx but direct benefits from the government. The more people you count in your community's census, citizen or not, the more benefits you will receive.

On the other hand, more people means a devaluation of the House of Representatives. Each congressperson in the House has the same number of constituents. Therefore, if the US population increases, the number of constituents per congressperson also increases, resulting in diminished political power per constituent. If we were to allow the population to decline and ameliorate the economic fallout, we would have increased political power per person for the House of Representatives. If every community has less people, and truly has less people not just declining to count certain populations, then the government benefits received would be proportional.

The Census is the government's guide to allocating funds to each district. If you live in an area where many non-citizens do not get counted in the Census, your community will receive less government support. If you have 200 people, you want funds for 200 people, not one hundred. Some might disagree and believe non-citizens shouldn't receive any form of government support. However, I implore you to remember government support is not simply food stamps and unemployment benefits. It is the funding for your schools, your roads, your social security, and so much more. So if your area has a large population of green card holders or permanent non-citizen residents and they are not counted, that means your children's schools will be comparatively underfunded, and you'll have a lot more potholes. More people equates to more money and power. Regardless of your political beliefs, you can be on board with that equation.

THE GOVERNMENT IS TRACKING YOU

Welcome to the twenty-first century, where everyone carries around a little device that doubles as their own personal tracker. Have you ever gotten into your car when the work day is done, and it automatically suggests the time it will take you to get home? Despite the fact that you didn't tell your phone where home was? Your phone knows that home is where you sleep and understands your trend of coming and going from work every day. Though I'm not one to freak out about the lack of privacy in the digital age, I would be more worried about your Apple products than a survey the government does every ten years.

There are a few valid fears surrounding the Census, and they should not be dismissed. They include concerns over immigration status and how data is stored and used. Some non-citizens may avoid the Census because their immigration status could potentially warrant deportation or other legal action. The Census Bureau shares information with other government departments like the Department of Homeland Security, but federal laws ensure the confidentiality of Census data. For example, the Census Bureau is not allowed to share individual responses; they can't tell ICE that Jane Doe lives at 222 Hope Lane. This means it is highly unlikely that responding to the Census would result in negative action against a non-citizen. These protections are in place to encourage an accurate count of the people living in the United States. Census data can only be used for statistical analysis and anyone who violates those laws can face fines up to $250,000 and up to five years in prison. Such high penalties discourage enumerators from divulging Census data to anyone. In terms of information security, answering the Census is safer than accepting cookies on a website or enabling location services on a smartphone.

GERRYMANDERING

Elected officials use Census data to draw district lines. This is actually mandated in the Constitution; gerrymandering is just an unfortunate byproduct. All US states redraw their congressional and legislative districts every ten years to ensure districts are equally populated. In 1920, there were 241,864 people per representative. One hundred years later each representative has 761,169 constituents. How we get to these numerically equal districts is via gerrymandering. Gerrymandering is the method of drawing political boundaries to give your party an advantage over the opposition. Elected officials from the state government draw the lines. This rule means that whatever party controls the state government can manipulate the districts to have a better chance of winning elections.

The simplest way to explain gerrymandering
is through this graphic:

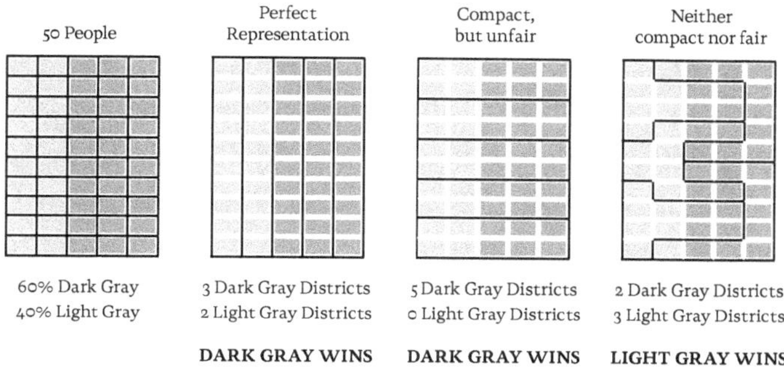

My home state of Texas has had a Republican governor since 1995, a Republican State Senate since 1997, and a Republican State House since 2003. This round will be the second redistricting in which Republicans have held a trifecta in the state government of Texas, meaning they can slice up districts however they so choose. To be clear, this happens on both sides of the aisle. Both parties are very guilty of gerrymandering. When the Census results come out, the party in power in your state can give themselves an election advantage for the next ten years. Some states have taken steps to combat gerrymandering, such as establishing independent commissions to draw districts. The Center for American Progress cites eight states that have such commissions: Washington, Montana, Michigan, California, Idaho, Colorado, Arizona, and Alaska. Voters should choose their politicians, not the other way around. When politicians choose their voters, we end up with a government that does not accurately represent the people's will. More work needs to be done to stop gerrymandering, but the Census is not to blame.

WHY SHOULD I FILL OUT THE CENSUS?

Kevin Iverson, North Dakota's Census Office manager, described not filling out the Census to the *Dickinson Press* as "ignoring and walking past a five-dollar bill every day for the next decade." That's passing up $18,250. North Dakota receives about $20,000 in federal funding for *each* person who fills out the Census. The money is used for education grants, supplemental nutrition assistance program (SNAP), highway planning and construction, and other benefits. The Project on Government Oversight (POGO) reports that the federal government uses the 2020 Census data to distribute 1.5 trillion dollars in annual spending in 316 federal programs. Filling out one survey helps decide how the United States government will spend fifteen trillion dollars over the next decade. It's not just about ensuring equal representation in congressional districts. It's about money.

The George Washington Institute of Public Policy at George Washington University put out a report titled, "Comprehensive Accounting of Census-Guided Federal Spending (FY2017)." It breaks down the federal spending for the fiscal year 2017 based on the data collected by the 2010 census:

- Texas: $101,606,495,000
- Georgia: $40,053,909,000

- North Carolina: $43,778,491,000
- Alaska: $4,889,633,000
- Rhode Island: $5,526,585,000.

Note: Alaska counted 710,231 people in the 2010 Census compared to Rhode Island's 1,052,567. Rhode Island counted 342,336 more people, which gave them $63,695,2000 more in annual funding than Alaska.

On April 1, 2020, many Americans celebrated Census Day by going online and filling out the Census questionnaire. Although it only comes once every ten years, it is often overshadowed by April Fool's Day. I filled out the Census on Census Day, mostly because I was stuck at home in the early phase of the pandemic, and between the banana bread recipes and Buzzfeed quizzes, it only seemed right to perform my civic duty and fill out the Census. If you don't fill it out on Census Day, there's still plenty of time to submit the online form before Census takers come knocking on your door. Home interviews usually begin between May 27 and August 14 of the Census year. The Census Bureau's mission is to count everyone, so they will send people to your home to get your responses. Of course, they aren't going to camp outside your home and wait for you. However, if you open the door to a Census taker, please comply with their questions; this is serious business. According to the American Bar Association, under federal law, refusal to answer all or part of the Census carries a hundred-dollar fine; there is a $500 fine for giving false answers.

After interviewing a sample of Gen Z and millennials on whether they participated in the 2020 Census, I realized some young adults aren't sure if they should be counted as part of their parents' household or on their own. Fill out the Census based on your household—the people you live with. Melody from Oklahoma recalled, "I didn't fill out the Census because when I asked my parents about it, they said they put me in theirs, so I didn't want to be counted twice." Parents, check with your kids if you include them in your questionnaire, and if not, a little reminder to fill out the Census can't hurt.

Another respondent, Diana from Florida, remarked that she was counted as part of her sorority house. Indeed, one house that is home to sixty or more girls is technically a household and can fill out one Census form together. An interesting note is that Diana's sorority is in California, not her home state of Florida. A student's "home" in terms of the Census is where they live while attending college. The Data Center, an independent analysis organization in southeast Louisiana put it simply, "If they're not living at their parents' home most of the time, the right place for them to be counted is in the town where they attend school. Students in college towns use local resources, including roads and public transportation. That's why they must be counted in those college towns."

The most common question I was asked when talking to Generation X and Baby Boomers about the Census was, "I own multiple properties in different states, so where should I count myself?" Whether it is a vacation home in North Carolina or a lake house in Utah—you don't fill the Census out twice. If that were the case, a specific section of the population would be counted multiple times. Instead, you fill out the Census based on where you live most of the time. My best advice for snowbirds that split their year fifty-fifty is to fill out the Census for the place that is home, not your second home. Even if we split our time evenly, one place always feels more like home than the other. However, you can indicate to the Census Bureau that you have additional properties with zero people living there through their website.

COUNT YOURSELF!

There are so many ways to fill out the Census. Whether you use the form in the mail, go online, or talk in person to a Census taker, make sure you get counted and counted in the right place. The simple fact of you existing in a particular state shapes how the government will serve you for the next ten years.

The bottom line, the Census ensures you have equal representation in Congress regardless of where you live. Whether you're in the boonies of West Texas or the heart of Atlanta, Georgia, each member of the House of Representatives has the same number of constituents. Second, it determines the funding your state will receive toward essential programs that support public health, local economy, and infrastructure. This funding builds up communities generating gains for years to come like a decrease in poverty and increase in quality of life for all residents. Third, politicians, businesses, and researchers use the data from the Census to inform their decisions. If your representative sees a population influx in your area, they could be more inclined to build a new park and recreation center there. If business leaders see more middle-aged people have concentrated in a particular suburb, they will open new branches of their companies there. So many elements that greatly affect our lives stem back to the Census.

If you didn't fill it out in 2020, don't miss out next decade.

PART 2

PRINCIPLES OF VOTERS AND NON-VOTERS

CHAPTER 8

HOPE, FEAR, ANGER, AND THE BRAIN

There's no crying in baseball.

When I was a kid, I played first base for our neighborhood softball team, and my dad was the coach. As the coach's kid, I felt the need to do just about anything to get on base. There is one game I vividly remember. We were down by two runs; my child-brain knew that the post-game snow cones tasted better when you won. I decided to lean into the next pitch and got pelted directly in my upper thigh. It stung so bad I immediately regretted that decision. Youth softball rules entitle a player hit by a pitch to an automatic walk to first base. Hopping over to the base with tears in my eyes, I looked at my dad, and he yelled, "Santora, pull it together! There's no crying in baseball." Of course, I hadn't seen the nineties movie *A League of Their Own* and thought my father had just come up with the most profound statement I'd ever heard. Fear and sadness were paralyzing emotions; if I had cried on first base that game, I'd have been useless to my teammates. Instead, I got angry and thought, *Well, I'm going to have a fat bruise regardless, so I better make this worth it.*

A decade later in November 2016, I was flipping through the news and saw *Duck Dynasty* star Willie Robertson on Fox Business. I was perplexed why they asked Willie about the country's reaction to Trump's victory and decided to watch the segment. They talked about the liberals crying because Trump won, and Willie said, "There's no crying in politics." There's no crying in politics? I interpreted this as him saying it was pointless for Democrats to feel deflated by the election result because it served them nothing but wasted energy. It got me thinking politics and baseball might not be so different. The anger that fueled me to steal second base might also have a place in politics. I learned there's no real crying in politics—but there are anger, hope, fear, and posturing.

I had the honor of speaking with Dr. Ann Crigler, a professor of political science and policy planning and development at the University of Southern California. Her research specialties include American politics, presidential elections, political communication, and emotions and politics. She's written on everything from election reform to emotion in political thinking, to the disputes over the 2000 election. Dr. Crigler is the expert of all experts, so I had to ask her: How do emotions affect politics and political campaigns? She explained there is a two-pronged approach to winning an election. "They [politicians] obviously focus on mobilizing their base, which requires a certain kind of enthusiasm and excitement about the candidate that you have to engender. Then there's, 'How do you kind of depress or suppress the opponent's voters so they don't feel like they have a lot of say? So why would they bother to go?'"

Immediately I thought of two candidates who nailed the first prong of mobilizing their base: JFK and AOC.

John F. Kennedy and Richard Nixon's head-to-head was the first televised presidential debate. Unlike previous debates, it wasn't just about someone's voice, but also what they looked like on television. JFK was a talented orator who was also dashingly handsome by almost all standards. By contrast, Nixon was nervously sweating and appeared meek. Voters flocked to JFK.

In modern times, AOC shares the lip color she uses on Instagram, and it sells out in two hours. Her words become TikTok trends (like when she confronted Representative Ted Yoho for calling her a bitch). Young women feel excited and empowered by her; they connect.

It goes deeper than just being handsome or having an iconic lip color. Both parties have used an emotional connection to win elections. Painting with broad strokes, Republicans use fear, and Democrats use hope. The two parties use both types of emotional connection, but Democrats often argue vague notions of a better future while Republicans promote specific elements to cause panic.

Bill Clinton used the word hope twelve times during his 1992 acceptance speech for the Democratic presidential nomination, proclaiming, "Let it be our cause that we give this child a country that is coming together, not coming apart, a country of boundless hopes and endless dreams, a country that once again lifts its people and inspires the world." He closed his speech, saying, "My fellow Americans, I end tonight where it all began for me: I still believe in a place called Hope." You have to admire the poetry of that last line, as Bill Clinton grew up in a small town called Hope, Arkansas. He tied together his hopes for the country to his humble beginnings in small-town America.

Barack Obama's 2008 campaign slogan was simply, "Hope." He referenced hope in every single one of his speeches on the campaign trail, and when accepting the nomination said, "I will restore our moral standing, so that America is once again that last, best hope for all who are called to the cause of freedom, who long for lives of peace, and who yearn for a better future." During his victory speech later that year, he stated, "Tonight we proved once more that the true strength of our nation comes not from the might of our arms or the scale of our wealth, but from the enduring power of our ideals: democracy, liberty, opportunity, and unyielding hope."

In contrast, Republican candidates have often focused on fear rather than hope. In George W. Bush's 2000 nomination acceptance speech, he promised, "We will confront the hard issues—threats to national security, threats to our health and retirement security—before the challenges of our time become crises for our children." He went on to say, "Our military is low on parts, pay, and morale. If called on by the commander in chief today, two entire divisions of the Army would have to report . . . Not ready for duty, sir." Hearing your country's army is not combat ready, especially when it has been known as a military superpower, was alarming, as it was intended to be.

Our forty-first president, George H. W. Bush, also engaged in the fear narrative in his nomination acceptance speech, emphasizing foreign policy, declaring "the Soviet

bear might be gone, but there are still wolves in the woods. We saw that when Saddam Hussein invaded Kuwait. The Mideast might have become a nuclear powder keg, our energy supplies held hostage. So we did what was right and what was necessary. We destroyed a threat, freed a people, and locked a tyrant in the prison of his own country." The message was of victory for the end of the Cold War, but also of prudence that many threats still loomed.

Boiled down to the most basic element, Republicans focus on security issues to gain favor, and Democrats emphasize inclusion to win hearts. Republicans want their government to show leadership and strength, and Democrats want their government to be subservient and compassionate. Realistically, a good government should have the best of both.

Here are three issues that demonstrate how fear and hope tango in American politics. Suspend your personal opinions for a moment, and instead, focus on how the opposing sides approach these challenges.

IMMIGRATION

In July of 2010, President Barack Obama spoke about comprehensive immigration reform. He highlighted how the United States is a nation of immigrants, emphasizing, "It is the constant flow of immigrants that helped to make America what it is. The scientific breakthroughs of Albert Einstein, the inventions of Nikola Tesla, the great adventures of Andrew Carnegie's US Steel and Sergey Brin's Google Inc.—all this was made possible because of immigrants."

Conversely, in a presidential campaign speech in 2016, Trump referred to immigrants and said, "They're bringing drugs, they're bringing crime, they're rapists." Naturally, hearing that people entering this great nation are here to tear it apart is a terrifying thought. Trump wanted to use that fear to make policies like intensified border restrictions and an expensive border wall necessary evils. His tactics worked and there was widespread support for his border policy among conservatives and moderates.

BATHROOM BILLS AND TRANSGENDER RIGHTS

Who can use which bathroom? Bathroom bills intended to give all people the right to use public restrooms matching their gender identify have been controversial at the state and local levels over the last decade. Republicans frequently argue that predators will follow women and girls into the bathrooms and assault them if these bills became law. Setting aside that a person can commit assault in a bathroom whether or not a "bathroom bill" becomes law—assault is scary. Progressives, on the other hand, argue that "bathroom bills" protect trans people from discrimination. In 2016, Texas Governor Greg Abbott weighed in on the issue, tweeting, "JFK wanted to send a man to the moon. Obama wants to send a man to the woman's restroom. We must get our country back on track." Democrats stuck to messaging that using the bathroom based on gender identity was a win for inclusion while Republicans insisted such laws would increase assaults against women.

This strategy is not confined to bathroom bills; Republicans have consistently used fear-mongering to gain support for restricting the rights of transgender people. Republicans want to bar transgender women and girls from competing with cisgender women in sports, stoking fears that girls would miss out on athletic scholarships and other recognition. The Associated Press contacted more than twenty legislators who sponsored bills written to restrict participation of transgender athletes in sports teams that match their gender identity and found that most of those lawmakers "cannot cite a single instance in their own state or region where such participation has caused problems." In fact, the 2020 Tokyo Olympics were the first to have transgender competitors, despite being able to participate since 2004. Researcher Joanna Harper estimates that out of 200,000 NCAA athletes, only about fifty are transgender.

Republican politicians tried to create a problem where one did not exist. Their fearmongering around transgender rights is completely unfounded, but unfortunately a portion of the population accepts this false reality. People tend to emphasize feelings over facts, which makes us susceptible to distorted hope and fictitious fear.

VOTING RIGHTS

Who can vote, and how? Americans are used to showing ID; we need ID to buy alcohol, drive a car, go through airport security, and even in the state of Texas, you need it to buy a gun. But neither party's rhetoric echoes these facts. Instead, President Trump tweeted allegations of election fraud starting in April 2020:

> *GET RID OF BALLOT HARVESTING, IT IS RAMPANT WITH FRAUD. THE USA MUST HAVE VOTER ID, THE ONLY WAY TO GET AN HONEST COUNT. . . . RIGGED 2020 ELECTION: MILLIONS OF MAIL-IN BALLOTS WILL BE PRINTED BY FOREIGN COUNTRIES, AND OTHERS. IT WILL BE THE SCANDAL OF OUR TIMES.*

Oppositely, Joe Biden tweeted in November 2020:

> *This is our moment to choose: Hope over fear. Unity over division. Science over fiction. Truth over lies. Vote.*

Another of his tweets from that same time said, "This is our moment to prove that love is more powerful than hate. Hope is more powerful than fear. Light is more powerful than dark. Vote before polls close." Biden plainly juxtaposed hope and fear, demonstrating his commitment to the hope narrative. Democrats followed this line of messaging of encouraging everyone to get out and exercise their rights.

Fear and hope produce different reactions. Fear pushes someone to seek additional information and ask questions like what's going on in my environment, how I assess this, and what I can control. Fear is a paralyzing emotion in many ways because it elicits a reactive response. Hope gives someone patience for the future and focuses on thoughts like "this will get better," "change is coming," and "we can do this." It's a link between stimulus and response.

The Fear-Hope Paradigm

Fear Stimuli	Criminals are crossing the border	Men are assaulting women in the bathroom	The election is being stolen
Fear Response	Want border control and harsher/ more closed immigration laws	Want bathroom bills that say you can only use the bathroom of your sex at birth	Stop the steal and do a complete audit. Potentially storm the Capitol
Hope Stimuli	We are a nation of immigrants, and immigrants have given so much to this country	People should have the right to use the bathroom of their gender identity	Everyone has the right to vote
Hope Response	Immigration still needs reform, but it will get better in time and immigrants are important to our country	Yes, we should support the LGBTQ community	The more people that vote, the more representative our democracy will be

ANGER AS A WEAPON

This leads us to the third emotion, anger. While hope and fear have their roles to play, anger takes center stage. Anger is the most mobilizing emotion, especially the anger of a collective group. A study from the University of Michigan on the impact of emotions on political behavior found that "anger in politics can play a particularly vital role, motivating some people to participate in ways they might ordinarily not—even if they have the ability and opportunity to do so.... Therefore, animating emotions, and the dynamic processes by which they are produced in each campaign, may powerfully alter electoral outcomes." Anger relies on the fuel of both hope and fear. People who have hope but don't see their visions becoming a reality get angry and take action. People who are afraid but believe they can overcome what they fear will get angry and take action. To rile people up, a candidate must give their side faith that they can be victorious. Conversely, a candidate wants to make his opponents' supporters feel hopeless and lose their cause.

President Donald Trump wielded all three emotions to secure his 2016 victory. According to Dr. Crigler, "He knows how to reach out and make people feel part of his team. And that sense of community is really important, especially in times that are kind of turbulent and isolating."

Trump's rhetoric consistently included the dangers of immigrants and the perceived weak security under the prior administration. He promised to save the country from such ills. Trump's rallies stirred up fear in many Americans, but they also gave them hope. His campaign had catchy slogans and phrases that spoke to a large portion of America that had felt left behind. Many of these people felt overlooked and wanted to go back to the way things used to be. They truly wanted to make America great again. While Trump supporters come from every race, creed, and state, he had a unique appeal to white Americans. A neighbor back in Texas told me, "[Trump] shares my values and my way of looking at the world. You can be white and prosper, and we have power."

Much of this sentiment is a reaction to the Obama years. The Obama administration pushed the country in a more progressive direction, and a black president deeply unsettled certain factions. No one can deny there was a considerable race dimension to this moment, and Trump cultivated anger from it to swing the pendulum back to his side. Trump demonized immigrants crossing the southern border, most of whom were not white, but remained silent on white applicants from countries that posed a threat to the United States, like Russia. The facts tell a different story. A State Department report from 2017 stated that a US citizen or legal resident has carried out every fatal terror attack on US soil since 9/11, not someone sneaking over our land border with Mexico or flying over from the Middle East. But the politics of our times are not rooted in fact. They feed off emotion.

Trump's brilliance is that he measured his rhetoric based on what would motivate his supporters to act. He was very selective in what was considered good or bad. While border security only meant the southern border, terrorism only meant foreign perpetrators. The Canadian border and domestic terror threats did not serve his goal. Trump derived loyalty from his supporters because he made people feel included and part of his team to make America great again. Coming from the business and entertainment world, he knew how best to communicate with people and make people feel part of his team.

Hillary Clinton attempted to channel the three emotions during her 2016 run, but she missed the mark. She was criticized for being too stiff or not feminine enough or too abrasive or weak—all very gendered condemnations.

People didn't like Hillary for other reasons, but would they tell a man he wasn't qualified to be president if he had served as a senator from New York and secretary of state? Especially if his opponent had never held political office? People didn't react because they had an in-depth understanding of Hillary's policies and disagreed; they just had a feeling about her. She needed to win over a plurality of people to defeat a limelight magnet like Trump, but she didn't. The people who loved her assumed everyone else would agree. The assumption of her victory ultimately hurt Hillary's campaign.

Trump's grip on the political sphere is still powerful, despite his removal from mainstream social media. Dr. Crigler noted how Trump uses fear tactics on other politicians within his party: "The Republicans are so fearful of Trump right now because they're afraid that they're going to be primaried by a Trump person." Think back to Madison Cawthorn pegging his opponent as a never-Trumper and then winning his race; it is a tactic proven viable. But it isn't just fear of Trump, but fear of dividing the Republican Party. Dr. Crigler explained, "It's very much a political question, and McConnell is a real key player here. McConnell doesn't particularly like Trump, is not a big Trump fan, but Trump is useful for advancing his agenda. He doesn't want to split the party because if he splits the party, then they lose power. So they're looking at the larger goals of power and how to regain control of Congress." Republicans need anger pointed in one direction, toward the Democrats. They can't afford to squabble among themselves, and they know that they can succeed under the Trump banner. Dr. Crigler continues, "The Republicans have actually situated themselves well because they have loaded up the judiciary; that was one of McConnell's biggest things, but they've also really done an excellent job of working with young people, to bring them into the party. And they have done an excellent job of training people to work at the local level. There's a lot of strength there."

ENTER THE BRAIN

Why do Republicans gravitate toward fear narratives and Democrats toward hope tropes? Paul Nail, a social psychologist from the University of Central Arkansas, offers an answer: "Conservatism, apparently, helps to protect people against some of the natural difficulties for living. The fact is we don't live in a completely safe world. Things can and do go wrong. But if I can impose this order on it by my worldview, I can keep my anxiety to a manageable level." The concept that conservative people desire a controlled environment that is safe for their preferred way of life helps us understand some of the policy chasms that divide the two parties. Someone seeking to control their environment and fears external threats will want a way to protect themselves, such as carrying a gun. If you believe criminals are entering the country through the Mexican border—hell, a firearm for personal protection seems like a great idea. Of course, there are plenty of liberal gun owners, but they don't necessarily share the same fears. The science is not saying conservatives are more afraid than liberals; it shows us conservatives are more reactive to fear. The physical makeup of the brain can make someone more reactive to fear-based stimuli.

A study from the University College of London found that students who identified as conservatives have a larger amygdala than those who identified as liberal. The amygdala is the part of the brain that processes "detection of threat and activation of appropriate fear-related behaviors in response to threatening or dangerous stimuli." Having a larger amygdala often means you could have a more heightened fear response. This means the way your brain developed, down to the size of its components, can affect your political views that are below your conscious understanding. It seems quite eerie, but it is a massive asset if wielded correctly. Conservatives who recognize their propensity to respond to fear and then assess the circumstances based on all of the facts can overcome negativity bias.

Across the aisle, liberals are less responsive to fear-based messaging due to some combination of smaller amygdalae and a lesser desire for order. A 2008 study published by the NIH to the National Library of Medicine studied participants with strong political beliefs and found that "individuals with measurably lower physical sensitivities to sudden noises and threatening visual images were more likely to support foreign aid, liberal immigration policies, pacifism, and gun control, whereas individuals displaying measurably higher physiological reactions to those same stimuli were more likely to favor defense spending, capital punishment, patriotism, and the Iraq

War." That study feels like it puts the entire partisan divide in a nutshell. I think of it as a political version of going cliff diving. If you're not afraid to dive off the metaphorical cliff, then you likely ascribe to policies that are pro-safety net. Meanwhile, if you're teetering on the edge, you want some assurances that this whole operation is safe and thus favor security-based policies.

Liberals often experience a positivity offset, a psychological term referring to the phenomenon where "neutral stimuli are viewed more positively, which can lead to exploratory behavior." People with this paradigm are more open to change and new experiences. Hence liberals support policies that challenge the status quo or expedite change. All too often, I see leftists wearing this champion of change as a badge of honor or pride rock on which to look down on conservatives. There is a ridiculous superiority complex among some liberals that is mostly unfounded. I have often heard liberal friends say, "I don't know why he thinks that way; he's smart" or "She just doesn't understand the impact of these policies." In fact, the work of Scott A. McGreal, a renowned psychology researcher from Australia, has found that conservatives' "lower openness to experience more likely reflects a preference for the familiar than simple-mindedness or lack of intellectual acuity."

We need to move away from the ad hominem dichotomy that all conservatives are uneducated hillbillies and that all liberals are socialist snowflakes. It is essential to our democracy to understand that the psychological differences between liberals and conservatives indicate what stimuli they respond most strongly to and how they are best persuaded to take a side.

FLIP THE SCRIPT, DEMOCRATIC FEAR AND REPUBLICAN HOPE

These are not absolutes; liberals are more receptive to conservative policies when there is a high level of fear. For example, in the wake of 9/11, the vast majority of the country was ready to go to war in the Middle East regardless of political affiliation. We were afraid and thus more willing to take a boots-on-the-ground approach instead of dallying over diplomacy. In 2001, a Gallup poll found that 88 percent of Americans approved of military action and invading Afghanistan. A supermajority of the American people was on board with war, partially because they were scared and wanted vengeance. It takes until 2013 for there to be a significant partisan divide over whether entering Afghanistan was the correct choice. Gallup tracked partisan opinions on the invasion and found that in 2013, 57 percent of Democrats thought it was a mistake compared to 30 percent of Republicans, and by 2019, 53 percent of Democrats thought it was a mistake compared to 25 percent of Republicans. The dip in disapproval between 2013 and 2019 can be attributed to the drawdown of troops that gave some hope that a positive end was in sight. The overall trend of approval waning as time passed could be best explained by the diminishing of the threat and restoration of the belief the United States was secure once again.

Conservatives' negativity bias held firm, perpetuating their belief that war was the answer, while liberals experienced a positivity offset as the shock wore off and retreated from their previous ideas. Conversely, conservatives can become more open to liberal policies in times they feel safe and secure. During periods of economic prosperity, conservatives are more likely to support welfare programs. In 2018, the people of Nebraska forced a referendum on Medicaid expansion while their elected officials advocated against it. The people of this deeply red state took matters into their own hands, and the Nebraska Initiative 427: Medicaid Expansion Initiative passed with 53.55 percent yes and 46.45 percent no.

That same year the people of Idaho and Utah took up similar initiatives because state leadership was refusing to support expanded Medicaid. Proposition 2 won 60.58 percent of the vote in Idaho for yes and 39.42 percent for no. Utah's referendum was called Proposition 3 and passed with 53.32 percent yes compared to 46.68 percent no. In the backdrop, the US economy grew 2.9 percent in 2018, just a hair shy of the Trump administration's 3 percent target. The economy was good, people were prospering, and thus social support programs were a bit more popular among conservatives. This change demonstrates that nothing happens in a vacuum, and the nuances of the conservative and liberal psyches are subject to influence by current circumstances.

ENTROPY RULES

The last question I asked Professor Crigler was one I'd been wrestling with for a while. Are Republicans more effective at reducing voter turnout than Democrats are at getting people to the polls? I wanted to know who was winning this political battle of emotions. When it comes down to votes cast and trends created, who has the high ground? She looked at me and leaned forward as if sharing a secret, and said, "Is it easier to get people to do nothing or to go positively do something? Entropy rules."

Back on that baseball diamond, I hoped we could win, I believed we were better than the other team, and I was angry the scoreboard didn't match what I thought to be true. Naturally, there was also a bit of fear my dad would be disappointed if we lost. Altogether this concoction drove me to quite literally take one for the team. The candidates that will win upcoming elections will be the ones who know how to play the game: The ones who use a combination of fear, hope, and anger to mobilize their base while creating an environment where the opposition's support feels like they are in an impossible uphill battle.

CHAPTER 9

BLUENECK AND OTHER POLITICAL IDENTITIES

If you could only introduce yourself to someone using a label, which one would you choose? It would be a tough decision because it's virtually impossible to pack the complexities of a full human being into one word. We have a multitude of labels that contribute to who we are as people.

We form our political identity through the accumulation of all our other labels. There are personal labels like race, gender, sexuality, religion, and education and group labels like family, sports affiliations, location, and companies. Labels help simplify how we interact with the world and can signal to others our values and beliefs.

Our instinct to use labels to simplify the world around us isn't completely wrong. It's usually safe to assume people vote the same as their parents; according to Gallup, 71 percent of teens hold the same views as their parents on social and political issues. But we have to remember it's not always the case. Locations aren't always the best indicator either; I'm from Texas, and I am by no means a far-right conservative. My political identity comes from the summation of my labels: Italian American, female, straight, Catholic, masters graduate, liberal mom and fiscally conservative dad, Patriots fan and day-one LAFC aficionado, and proud Texan. I decided I wanted to tell the stories of people whose list of labels adds up to an unexpected political identity. We make too many assumptions and develop animosity for those who don't think exactly like us without stopping to consider why they might hold a different opinion. I hope these stories build your political empathy and help us stop demonizing the opposing side. At the end of the day, we are all Americans, and we all want our country to succeed. We just have different ideas of how to get there.

THE BLUENECK

First is a rising country music star, Chris Housman. I had the honor of hearing his story firsthand. Housman grew up on a farm in Kansas near a town of only 200 people. He started performing nineties country songs at the age of seven. Maybe it was the songs' themes of glorification of one specific way of life or maybe it was what the music didn't say, but something wasn't quite right. The lyrics didn't feel authentic to him. It's not like he didn't fit in; he was homecoming king and loved by his community. Growing up watching Fox News, he began to think, "I don't love Bill O'Reilly, and the things he's saying don't make sense to me." I asked him about how his community discussed politics when he was a kid: "it wasn't something that people talked about, it was so deeply rooted that it's just the way things were … the kids in my class would have all identified as Republicans and George Bush lovers because that's what their parents were; there's no other option." He always felt there had to be something more out there and would come to realize, "Some people just need exposure to a life different from what they had access to growing up."

Housman would cross that bridge when he moved to Tennessee for college, but first, he took a different kind of leap. The summer after high school, he came out to his parents as gay: "I sat my mom and dad down and initially my mom was like, 'You're not gay; this is just a phase.' But then she said, 'It's fine, just don't tell anybody.' The thing is, it's not something I need to be ashamed of, and I had already begun to tell people in my small town." If you know anything about small-town life, it's that the gossip mill is faster than the pony express. Housman realized, "She didn't have an issue with it at first until she found out people were finding out. . . . Conservatism is so deeply ingrained that she was so focused on what other people would think because it wasn't the norm in our town."

The singer/songwriter became publicly gay in 2008, before the Supreme Court legalized gay marriage and before many anti-discrimination laws were in place. He felt, "I can't really do [country music] and be myself, as this newly openly gay person. . . . The first song I put out was a pop song." This still didn't feel authentic, so he stepped away from music for several years.

Eventually, he returned and began writing country again. "I had put out two or three songs previously that are just kind of, more middle-of-the-road country songs." They are excellent songs; I love the single "Long Story Long." His career took a turn when he asked himself, "Why is an entire genre of music excluding all these people? How did we get here?" Housman began researching the history of country music and its roots in promoting a particular small-town lifestyle without room to step outside the norm. He also discovered the contributions of people of color to this southern style of music that history erased and became aware of just how narrow the net of inclusion was cast in this genre. Armed with information and renewed self-confidence, Housman began writing a new song titled "Blueneck."

I implore you to open up Spotify or Apple Music and stream his song right now. Blueneck is a word Chris Housman coined and is a term for a person from a red state that ascribes to liberal or progressive political ideals. The song opens like a typical country song; there's corn and a reference to civil liberties. Housman wanted to ensure his lyrics weren't "bashing Republicans or conservatives, or even rednecks really. Instead I wanted to shine a light on how country music can be more inclusive."

The internet exploded as TikTok users began using the sound in their videos and comments kept rolling in about how people deeply connected with his song. It was in the top ten on the American iTunes Chart when it was released. Of course, not everyone is going to love a left-leaning country song. To my surprise, when I asked

Housman about the backlash to the song, he said, "The main thing people are saying is 'This isn't country.' Well, yes it is."

"Blueneck" is a true country song. I have to commend Housman's lyrical genius; he was able to address challenges faced by women, people of color, and members of the LGBTQ community in such a way that the only criticism was, "Well, that's not country." For Housman and his fans, country music is for everybody and should be just as inclusive.

Speaking with the rising star, you can feel how deep his empathy runs. Housman has also been involved in local politics doing grassroots organizing for Democrat candidate Keeda Haynes's 2020 run for Tennessee's Fifth Congressional District. He has begun to enjoy local politics because he sees it as an opportunity to bring people together to make effective change. He describes himself very accurately, "I've always wanted to make sure everybody in a room feels included or seen. . . . I used to get super anxious if we have a reservation for six people, but a seventh person is coming because what if they don't have a chair or feel like they are invading the group. . . . That's just ingrained in how my brain works." He's using the overwhelmingly positive reaction to his song "Blueneck" to capitalize on his mission for inclusion in country music and has more songs coming out soon.

Housman's story is an important reminder that if you know a few labels about someone, you know a few labels about them.

THE SCIENTIST

Moving to the East Coast, I'd like to introduce you to Joy Atkins, a nurse who also teaches at Rutgers University.

Joy describes her hometown in south Jersey as "very, very country." Growing up, her parents would turn on the news in the evenings but never directly discuss politics at home. Joy reflected that her family generally held the same political opinions, but, she says, "I was the first of my siblings to go to college, and I think that's what makes me different from them. Part of it is my personality, but when I want an answer, I go look for the answer that is supported by research and evidence, not the answer that I hope it is. My siblings get a lot of their information from the news or one newspaper. I seek out different sources to support the information I see." In a time where mountains of disinformation pile up on social media and even some traditional news sources, it is essential to fact-check.

Today, Joy teaches a class at Rutgers University to nursing students about disinformation in public health. She believes that when it comes to public health, politics has no place in the equation. "It's about the science, not what any Democrat or Republican says we should do. In this case, they aren't the experts; they need to listen to the experts." Her approach to politics is "follow the science." It is what she does when examining public health decisions and as a method of consuming information. She takes care to only absorb information from reputable sources and teach her children and students to do the same. Joy has had a few unvaccinated students in her classes say she's pro-vaccine because she's a Democrat. In reality, it's the other way around, because she's a nurse and understands the benefits of vaccination and therefore supports political candidates who act in the best interest of public health. This instance is not the first time people have made assumptions about Joy.

"I remember when people were saying Colin Powell could run for president. And they said, 'You're black; you're gonna vote for the black guy.' And I'm like, 'No, that's not gonna make me vote for him; that's not how that works.' I'm not gonna vote for somebody based on their skin color." In her view, people make quick assumptions because they haven't been exposed to other ideas or someone they trust told them this is how it works. She recalled President Trump's failed lawsuit against New Jersey in the wake of the 2020 election: "On Facebook, high school classmates who still live in that area [southern New Jersey] were saying how did he lose New Jersey. Like, there are Trump signs everywhere, like, 'Hello, there's more to this state than just that tiny town. Come up to North Jersey and see for yourself.'"

Joy's wish is that younger people will continue to realize their ability to make their country a better place. She said, "It wasn't until later in life when I really recognized the importance of speaking up and having your voice heard; voting is the easiest way to do that." We can all learn from her evidence-driven approach to politics and that it's never too early to get involved. We must understand that just because one or two labels matches with a politician doesn't automatically mean they are voting for them.

Seattle, Washington, has often been called the most liberal city in America or the bluest place in the United States. It is also the place Wilson, a staunch Republican, calls home. Naturally, one of my first questions was whether people made assumptions about his political beliefs based on his labels. He recited back to me, "I am an Asian American bisexual male in Seattle; everybody thinks I'm a snowflake liberal. [They] have a hard time wrapping their heads around the idea that the Republican Party would appeal to someone like me, but it does." With that cue, I asked him to share what he wished people would take the time to understand about his political views. Wilson said, "I believe in limited government, and I don't think we should have hundreds of social welfare programs; that kind of help should be from the community, not DC. I'd rather give my unemployed neighbor a job at my company than be taxed that same amount to pay for their unemployment benefits. People assume all Republicans don't want to help anyone but themselves, maybe that's true for some wazzus, but the Republicans I know have big hearts; they just have an alternate idea on how to do things."

"I can see people tense up when I say I voted for a local Republican; sometimes they think it's a joke, but it is obvious they think I'm out of my mind. My moderate friends who know me know that my weekends are spent at our local charities, but I shouldn't have to explain myself every time. It's like I have to say, 'I'm Republican, BUT.' You don't have any Democrats saying that around here—and they probably don't think the exact same as their other liberal friends, but they don't talk about it; they just assume they're all on the same page. I mean, how do we get anywhere if we don't talk to each other about the biggest issues facing our society?"

Wilson's point of view makes a lot of sense. Many people can relate to his frustrations, but I wanted to know how he became Republican, especially since his parents weren't politically active. He recalled that it all started at a party in his twenties just after George H. W. Bush lost the 1992 election. "Somebody was making a toast to Bill Clinton and was drunkenly reciting some of his biggest policy proposals, and I just stood there thinking, *Wait what*? I don't agree with half of that stuff." Wilson didn't vote in the 1992 election, but he hasn't missed one since then. "It all sort of snowballed from there. I started reading the newspaper—we didn't have smartphones back then—so I physically read the paper and put some energy into what was going on around me, especially on the local level because that's where I could see the change happening or not happening, for better or for worse."

He was adamant he would never leave Seattle unless his family needed to; he has taken on this role of being his community's resident Republican. While he disagrees with his Democrat friends on most policy issues, he feels the increased polarity in the US political system is highly counterproductive. "I've seen politicians on both sides that refuse to negotiate or just say stupid things that make you just want to shake them 'til the candy comes out." He's frustrated that constituents sometimes pull away from their political leaders when they reach across the aisle to pass policy: "That's their job; the reason nothing happens in Congress unless one party has a supermajority is that politicians are so afraid to be seen as moderate or sympathetic to the other side, people forget that at the end of the day there are no sides we all live in this country."

His message to other Seattleites and people who live in politically homogenous communities is direct: "Don't just accept what everyone around you is doing or voting for, and if jumping into the whole political thing seems like too much, just pay attention to the local stuff like mayor and city council." I couldn't agree more.

LISTEN BEYOND THE LABEL

Take a moment to reflect on your political affiliation; if someone only knew one of your labels, would they guess it correctly? And even if they got it right, would they know where on that area of the political spectrum you associate? We can't expect others to understand our ideology from a bit of information, so we shouldn't try to fill in the gaps in their beliefs when we don't know much about them.

I found common political ground with all of the people I interviewed for this book. None of them matched my labels. If we take a moment to listen to what someone believes and why they believe it, we might realize there's a lot more that makes us similar than sets us apart. And if we all turn around and vote, we'll be represented by people who understand that too.

I hope we can learn from Chris that just because a genre or activity has been dominated by one type of person doesn't mean we can't jump in. From Joy, I hope we remember to question everything, from what we believe to where we get our information to why we make assumptions about others. And from Wilson, I hope we do not forget to talk to each other even when we disagree, because it's from that place we can begin to understand one another.

PART 3

CULTIVATING THE VOTE

CHAPTER 10

ONE HUNDRED-PLUS YEARS OF VOTER ENGAGEMENT

I wish people in this country voted in elections with the same fervor as Texas high school students did when selecting homecoming court. My friend Lauren was our homecoming queen senior year, and she was the perfect choice. She checked all the boxes—beautiful, intelligent, and kind. I think we had 99 percent participation in that vote.

Half of those people probably don't vote regularly.

At one point, we knew the power of voting; selecting a homecoming queen in the South is no small feat. But somewhere between high school graduation and the next election, we forgot about the agency we intrinsically hold. The hallways would be abuzz with students asking, "Did you vote yet?" Group chats would ding that only a few hours were left to cast ballots, and lunch was filled with discussions on who you voted for and why. Of course, we had no barriers to voting. We voted at school, where we were five days a week, and the energy around the vote created a deep desire to connect that drove even the most unengaged students to the ballot box.

I wish I could capture the excitement of that Friday night before the football game when the homecoming court takes the field to await the crowning of king and queen. The stadium lights are almost too bright, and everyone marvels at the girls in stilettos walking across the turf. Trust me; it was feigned confidence. We had bets on who would fall; thankfully, no one had to suffer such public embarrassment. Standing in a neat row, we all held our breath. When the announcer said Lauren's name, we hollered and clapped until our hands hurt. I want to bottle up that energy and distribute it at the beginning of each election cycle.

THE LEAGUE OF WOMEN VOTERS

If you want to know how to become a homecoming queen, ask a girl from Texas. If you want to know how to educate America on voting, ask the League of Women Voters. According to their website, the League of Women Voters (LWV) envisions "a democracy where every person has the desire, the right, the knowledge, and the confidence to participate." They work to "register voters, provide voters with election information through voter guides as well as candidate forums and debates. LWV was founded in 1920, six months before the Nineteenth Amendment was passed, and has been advocating for voting rights ever since. Today they have over 700 state and local groups that carry out their mission. Their work is nonpartisan and reaches every corner of our democracy. While the group was initially formed for women, they altered their charter in 1973 to include men. In 2020 alone, they protected over twenty-five million voters in over seventy lawsuits, educated over six million voters on their website VOTE411.org, supported 233,000 people in registering to vote, and covered specific information on over 22,000 political races. I wanted to take a look inside their institution and see how we could learn from their success.

LESSONS FROM 2020

I sat down (albeit virtually) with Jeanette Senecal, the Senior Director of Mission Impact for the League of Women Voters. She joined the League in 1999 and has worked on everything from the organization's VOTE411.org website to modernizing election laws and expanding civic engagement. Given her history with the organization, I had to know how the 2020 election cycle changed their strategy and what lessons they would take moving forward.

Senecal remarked it's "hopefully something we won't live through again. But it did teach us multiple lessons. . . . Our schedule for voter education will forever be changed as voters are now looking for information on registration, early voting, and absentee ballots all at once. . . . Our resources really need to provide that information all the time, and it needs to be updated constantly, with state-specific, even locally specific information."

Millions of Americans voted for the first time in 2020, all of whom were navigating a challenging voting environment. However, the nature of the pandemic lowered many of the usual barriers. More citizens had access to mail-in voting than ever before, which helped increase participation. Senecal said that for the 2022 and 2024 elections cycles, their "advocacy strategies and work with elections officials need to focus on helping voters use the vote by mail process." She was clear that "this doesn't mean we want to limit in-person voting options because maintaining in-person voting options is very important to maintaining accessibility and protecting the civil rights of different groups, including people with disabilities and people that require language assistance."

Voting needs to be accessible to those who are eligible to participate, but fewer restrictions on mail-in voting are very controversial. In the 2020 cycle, states where you needed to have notaries or witnesses waived the requirement due to the pandemic. We also have learned that the mere perception of voter fraud can spur insurrection. Thus, there needs to be a balance between accessibility, security, and perceived security. Senecal made an important point about what we should take away from 2020's increased participation: "It showed that people really want to participate and that the barriers are sometimes in the system and it has nothing to do with the people … if we can meet the needs of the voters instead of trying to make voters meet the needs of the system, we can continue to see this kind of great turnout in elections." She also remarked, "Mail-in voting is a critical component of the options that voters need to make voting fit their needs and lifestyle, but it can't be the only opportunity. . . . We have to maintain in-person voting." According to the Pew Research Center's 2020 analysis, 46 percent of people voted by mail. Fifty-eight percent of Biden voters used the mail option compared to 32 percent of Trump voters. Almost half of the voting population used a mail-in ballot, demonstrating that in-person and by-mail voting are essential parts of our voting system.

We understand how each party communicates with its constituents with appeals to fear, hope, and anger. But a nonpartisan organization like LWV doesn't play those games. I asked how their organization targets their rhetoric for different audiences—frequent voters versus new voters. I thought that people who voted consistently didn't need the same type of information as someone who hadn't before, but I was wrong. Senecal clarified, "Many experienced voters were actually first-time voters themselves [in 2020] because they were voting using a new method. So even with an experienced voter, we don't want to assume they don't need the basic information that a first-time voter does . . . [especially] if they have moved to a new state."

She explained that in terms of logistics, experienced and new voters need the same information. However, when it comes to the why behind voting, new voters are the ones who need the extra push. LWV seeks to educate these voters, regardless of their political leanings, on "the why, what's at stake, why it is important for them to participate, what these elected officials do, how the decisions they make will affect voter lives—specifically tying it back to education, job security, environmental justice, and other issues people already connect to." Frequent voters don't need these incentives explained because they already know why they participate and consistently exercise their right to vote.

CHALLENGES TO VOTER ENGAGEMENT

Now the question becomes: How do we get all of this information into the right hands? 2020 was LWV's most extensive social media marketing and education campaign ever, and it has become a cornerstone of their communication. They have found the right balance between social media blasts and person-to-person, also called relational organizing. Instead of putting out a series of PSAs or information-dense content, they focus on creating shareable material—aesthetically pleasing posts that people can share in their Instagram stories and Facebook feeds. Having people spread accurate information within their personal network is very effective in broadening the reach of their educational materials. They focus on social media to target specific markets and communicate on the community level. Since LWV is a federated organization, they have thousands of people who can help spread the correct information to their specific neighborhoods in all fifty states.

The League has also made a conscious effort to reach Spanish-speaking voters. In 2020, they partnered with the National Association of Latino Elected and Appointed Officials (NALEO) to translate VOTE411.org into Spanish for the very first time. Over 80,000 VOTE411 users accessed the Spanish-language content for a combined 388,876 page views, according to the Election Impact Report. They also produced Spanish language social media ads in Florida, Georgia, Nevada, New York, Pennsylvania, and Texas. But LWV didn't stop there. They also made sure to cover radio and paper communication just like they do for English language content. They send over half a million bilingual postcards to citizens in Florida, New York, and Texas. Then, in the final weeks of the election cycle, they invested in Spanish radio ads on iHeart Radio, which reached over two million people in eleven states. These efforts are essential to democratizing the voting process as 13 percent of the United States, just over forty-three million people, speak Spanish as their first language, according to Babbel. It is worth pointing out that enough people in the US speak fluent Spanish to make it an official language.

IT SHOULDN'T BE PARTISAN TO WANT EVERYONE TO VOTE

What I find to be maybe the most impressive about The League of Women Voters is not their massive reach or the diligence of their work, but rather their ability to remain nonpartisan for over one hundred years. World Wars have come and gone, presidents assassinated, civil unrest rising and falling again—and not once did they promote a political party or candidate. They have engaged in promoting specific policies like campaign finance reform but believe that is an extension of their drive to protect the vote. In a blog post on the organization's website in February 2021, CEO Virginia Kase Solomon made their position clear, "The League of Women Voters of the United States is proud to be nonpartisan, neither supporting nor opposing candidates or political parties at any level of government, but always working on vital issues of concern to members and the public."

Of course, the League has been accused of partisanship from time to time, primarily due to their advocacy work in expanding franchise access. Solomon does not shy away from these accusations: "Supporting the democratic processes of registering eligible voters and casting and counting ballots is seen by some as subverting one political party, even though these are sacred tools of our democracy. Likewise, empowering voters who previously have been left out of the process and supporting the anti-racism movement does not mean we are in alliance with one ideological segment of American government; rather, it means we are doing what we were founded to do: Stand[ing] up for what is right." This statement particularly hits home for me because I am so frustrated by the partisan divide over the right to vote.

While sitting in the midst of what feels like a hyper-polarized society, it can be challenging to think that we share a similar endgame, especially when some politicians are pushing for an increase of barriers to voting. Yet Senecal makes an optimistic point: "The vast majority of Americans believe that people should be able to choose their politicians and that their politicians should represent them. . . . They think we should be making voting safe and accessible for everybody, we share common values as Americans, and we think we should be guaranteeing the right to vote because we know it impacts key decisions that affect our life. . . . They believe we should make the promise of democracy real for everyone."

VOTER ENGAGEMENT IS CRUCIAL

We should make the promise of democracy real for everyone. We have to. LWV proves this happens at the local level, and being a nonpartisan advocate for voting rights is possible. The mistake we make is focusing too much on how voting changes could affect elections. We dive into how Democrats would win more often if communities of color voted consistently or how specific voting methods are more often used by one party, so restricting them could affect election results. That's the wrong message. We should be focusing on full participation because, at the end of the day, we want a government that truly represents us. If communities of color don't vote, their needs won't be represented. If working class people don't have extended hour voting options and therefore can't vote, their needs won't be represented. If their needs aren't represented, we end up with a frustrated and angry society that becomes opposed to the system of government rather because their government doesn't speak for them. Senecal puts it eloquently: "What you're really looking to do is enfranchise everybody, no matter our race, background, or zip code, we believe that our democracy should work for all of us. . . . Whether you're independent, Democrat, Republican, the majority of voters believe that our system should work for the people."

Moving forward, LWV will continue to focus on organizing and building community-based power alongside initiatives for diversity, equity, and inclusion. Senecal described people as their silver bullet, and I couldn't agree more. When people show up and participate, we all benefit. Whether it's submitting testimony for redistricting, writing letters of concern to representatives, or simply voting, people have the power. We sometimes forget democracy is not static; it does not exist merely because of our existing constitution nor our nation's history. It is dynamic and must consistently be protected by the people who desire to live within it. We protect our ability to choose our leadership when we actively vote for our leaders. We protect our fellow citizens when we actively ensure they, too, can vote for our leaders. And we protect our future when we educate our communities on how to participate in our democracy.

The League of Women Voters website provides a variety of services: an easy search to find your current elected officials; VOTE 411, which is a one-stop shop for everything from registration to candidate information to voting; and countless education materials on voting rights, redistricting, and how to get involved with a local chapter. Though the organization was initially founded by women and for women, today it represents all Americans. No matter your race, gender, religion, or party affiliation, it is a welcoming space with accurate information. I fully endorse their work and encourage you to share their materials with the voters, new and old, in your community.

CHAPTER 11

THE SINGLE-ISSUE VOTER

When I was a kid, I loved looking for seashells on the beach. I would walk the shoreline for hours to find the perfect patterns and colors. Everyone else would be sunbathing or splashing in the waves or chasing off seagulls, and I would be head down, eyes locked on the tiny treasures waiting where the sea meets the shore. One time, I was so focused on looking for violet shells, trying to get a full rainbow spectrum of color, that I didn't notice I had walked into the middle of a pickup game. I was pegged in the right temple with a football and knocked flat on my rear end. I was stunned more than anything, and some overly buff college frat star ran over to make sure I was okay. I learned nothing from that incident because I got back up, brushed off some sand, and went right back to looking for purple shells. This is what it is like to be a single-issue voter. There is one focus, and it causes people to willfully ignore external stimuli, like the football, that could be dangerous to their best interests.

A single-issue voter decides who they are going to vote for based solely on one policy. One of the most common is pro-life versus pro-choice. Many devout Christians vote for pro-life politicians because they believe any form of abortion directly conflicts with their Christianity, and they must prevent others from engaging in such behavior. Thus, they will categorically not vote for any politician who is pro-choice, even if they align with that candidate on every other issue.

Another example is the fiscal voter; they only vote on policies that benefit their field of business or lower their taxes without regard for social programs or other issues. These people vote for whoever will create a system that will help their company make the most money, usually in the form of tax cuts and decreases in regulations.

An increasingly popular form of single-issue voting is on gun control. People will vote for politicians that support constitutional carry or candidates who want to increase gun regulations dramatically. Think back to the cheers Beto O'Rourke got for telling everyone he would take their AR-15s, and then he promptly became irrelevant in the Democratic primary.

There are also single-issue voters who are not always in the limelight, like immigration and health care. Many people who either have pre-existing conditions or family members with those afflictions seek candidates who protect their right to health care. DACA recipients and their families naturalized as citizens vote for candidates who protect their status in the United States. They wouldn't support a candidate who threatened DACA because that sort of policy could result in their deportation. It makes sense that specific issues have a dominant role in someone's decision-making process. If something affects your lifestyle, you're more likely to focus on it. However, ignoring other issues in favor of a single policy can be a dangerous game to play. Nothing happens in a vacuum, and single-issue voters should be encouraged to take a more holistic look at politics.

PRO-BIRTH VERSUS PRO-LIFE VERSUS PRO-CHOICE

Growing up in the Bible Belt, I am highly familiar with the pro-lifer. What I have learned from being steeped in the "life begins at conception" ideology is that you have to meet people where they stand. Approaching a pro-lifer and saying they should vote for a pro-choice candidate because they match their values on every other policy will not work. Instead, you have to determine if they are genuinely pro-life or simply pro-birth. Someone who is genuinely pro-life is more likely to accept information on other policies that protect the sanctity of life, such as foster care programs, protections for domestic violence victims, and accessible health care. Never approach this saying, "You're not really pro-life if you don't support this policy." That is only going to get your entire argument dismissed. Instead, demonstrate that you value their pro-life beliefs and how they are congruent with other policies.

Unfortunately, a section of the pro-lifers aren't really pro-life; they are pro-birth. Pro-birth, a term I like to use to separate those who want control over women's bodies rather than protect life, means that they just want the babies to be born but don't invest in what happens after the child comes into the world. From my experience, it is near impossible to reason with a pro-birther. I once found myself arguing with a man who believed in small government and that vaccines shouldn't be required because "we have dominion over our bodies" but thought that abortion at any point for any reason should be a felony. The irony was lost on him.

THE FISCAL VOTER

"I'm socially liberal but fiscally conservative" is a standard answer people give on their political stance. It exudes some sense of "I don't hate any particular group, but also I care about money the most." Speaking to the fiscal voter needs to tie everything back to wealth. Take immigration; if you tell a fiscal voter they should care about immigration policy because of the people seeking refuge from abusive regimes and drug cartels, they will not empathize. It doesn't make them bad people; it just doesn't captivate their attention. You can't speak emotions to someone who thinks in dollar signs. Instead, talk about immigration policy in the context of financial gain.

I spoke with a man from Orange County, California. His hometown and Ivy League pedigree were made apparent from the moment I met him. We spoke in the weeks following the 2020 election, and he admitted he had voted for Trump again. He said in a whisper, "Well, you know I voted for Trump twice; he really gets the economy." In the next breath, he proceeded to state, "It is so stupid that my friend can't get a work visa. She is a huge asset to the tech sector." I attempted to connect the dots between voting for an anti-immigration candidate and being upset when a colleague faces deportation. He said, "Well that's why I can't tell her who I voted for. She would be hurt." We began discussing his other political beliefs, which didn't seem to match up with the candidate he had chosen. I asked, "Why did you vote for President Trump if you're only on board with his anti-China economic policies?" He paused for a moment and said, "Without a strong economy, nothing else matters."

I shared with my West Coast friend a bit of information on the economic impacts in his backyard: In 2017, Santa Barbara County struggled with labor shortages due to a lack of migrant workers and had to leave thirteen million dollars' worth of crops to rot in the field. The inflow of labor from abroad has drastically slowed, not just for farmhands; the search for skilled talent is the top concern for 89 percent of executives in the manufacturing business, according to the National Law Review.

Telling this fiscal voter that current immigration policy is letting millions of dollars go to waste, creating an unnecessary barrier to talent acquisition, and could force firms to send work abroad made his eyes narrow. I could tell he was thinking about his friend on the verge of deportation. He shook his head and said, "Well, I really didn't think of it like that, but I'm still proud I voted for Trump." Of

course, one conversation will not wholly change someone's mind.

THE BIG GUNS

Texans own around fifty-one million firearms, which is
more guns than owned by the 300 million people who
make up the fifteen nations of the European Union. Texans own the most guns in the United States, and we like
to flaunt that fact, especially in front of Oklahoma. It
is safe to say you will never convince a proud firearms
owner to vote for a candidate who proposes gun control
legislation. However, pretty much every Republican in
Texas primaries is for constitutional carry or protecting
the Second Amendment to some level. This means there's
quite a bit of room for other issues to come into play.

The goal would be to convince the AR-15 aficionado to
look further into the gun-wielding candidates to see their
other policies. Take the Texas Fifth District's 2018 primary between Lance Gooden and Bunni Pounds. Both
are Republicans who are firm supporters of gun liberties.
However, while Pounds is categorically against gay marriage and believes the only recognized union should be
between a man and a woman; Gooden only goes as far
as to say that adoption agencies should be able to disal-
low LGBT adoptions. If you're opposed to total equality
for gay couples but do think they have a right to civil
union, then Gooden would be your logical choice. Lance
Gooden had the backing of the Young National Republicans Federation and won the Fifth District. Primary
elections are an opportunity for single-issue voters to

be educated on other policies and vote accordingly; it is too late if you wait until the general. Because it is more than likely, you'll end up in a situation like Beto's 2018 senate run where option A is gun rights Ted Cruz, and the alternative is gun control Beto. A single-issue voter isn't going to see anything else.

HEALTH IS WEALTH

Calling the Affordable Care Act "Obamacare" was quite the blunder. It's like if the No Child Left Behind Act was called Bush-education. Nonetheless, the Affordable Care Act is vital to families who might not otherwise have health insurance. According to the Department of Health and Human Services, thirty-one million people are currently covered under the legislation and don't want to see this disappear. An essential provision of the act is that health insurance companies cannot refuse to cover you or charge you more just because you have a pre-existing condition. Eighty-six percent of Americans between the ages of fifty-five and sixty-four have a pre-existing condition, which might lead you to believe these conditions come with age, but it affects the entire population. A 2017 CNN analysis found that the ten most common pre-existing conditions for Americans include acne, anxiety, diabetes, asthma, sleep apnea, depression, COPD, extreme obesity, atherosclerosis, and cancer. Having cystic acne as a teenager is bad enough; there's no need to upcharge someone for basic health care over it too.

Health care can be costly, so it's not hard to imagine that someone would make voting decisions based on who might protect their access to health care. My mom has lupus, an auto-immune disease that is a pre-existing condition. I want her to have access to the best health care, so I would never vote for a candidate that wanted to reverse those protections. While I don't consider myself a single-issue voter, if someone wanted me to think beyond just the Affordable Care Act, it would make sense to talk to me about a topic related to health. Some consider abortion access as health care, so reaching out to a single-issue health care voter about pro-life and pro-choice policies could be the best avenue to capture their attention. You could argue both sides: "Since you're so invested in health care, what about this candidate who also protects a woman's right to her body, which is also health care" or "I know you're invested in the Affordable Care Act, and all life should be protected regardless of pre-existing conditions, just like all babies should be protected."

Think back to AOC's primary race against Joseph Crowley for the New York Fourteenth. Both candidates support the Affordable Care Act, but Crowley voted yes on banning partial-birth abortions. Meanwhile, AOC is vehemently pro-choice and has told 10 WBNS, a CBS News affiliate, that abortion bans are a "brutal form of oppression" centered on "owning women." Instead of waiting for the general election to just vote for whichever side will protect the Affordable Care Act, a single-issue health care voter could be educated on related subjects and thus see a benefit in engaging in the primary process.

The last type of single-issue voter we will address is immigration. Coming from the state with the longest border with Mexico, I have heard just about every position on the topic. Immigration is a complex subject; there's the border wall (or lack thereof), DACA, refugee status, sanctuary cities, pathways to citizenship, chain migration, the diversity lottery, ICE, the infamous Muslim ban, birthright citizenship, and so much more. The first step would be determining what part of immigration policy this person or group of people is most dedicated to and connect that point to other issues. What would you talk to them about if you wanted to engage a single-issue voter to act on topics other than immigration? For example, if someone is anti-immigration because they fear foreigners might enter and try to harm US citizens, talk to them about homeland security policies that keep us safe and which candidates keep national security a priority.

If they are pro-immigration for financial reasons, like the farmer shortage mentioned previously, you might talk to them about pro-business candidates. If they are pro-immigration for human rights reasons, you might speak with them about pro-life issues since they already have a connection to the idea of the sanctity of human life.

After the fall of Kabul, a tidal wave of Americans reached out to help with the evacuation and resettlement of Afghan refugees. Refugee Services of Texas had a massive influx of new volunteers; I attended one of their virtual training sessions for the Dallas office, alongside almost three hundred other people. Toward the end of the call, one woman from Highland Park (a very wealthy neighborhood in Dallas) shared, "Though I have always voted against mass immigration, I am here to volunteer because I am pro-life and what those women will go through if they are left to the Taliban is against the convictions in my soul."

That one sentence told a whole story of its own. Here is a woman living a life of privilege who has suddenly empathized with refugees because of their plight's connection to her pro-life ideals. This type of moment doesn't need a significant humanitarian crisis to be its catalyst. We can create these links when we listen to the person's beliefs and the why behind those stances.

Keep in mind this isn't always a straight shot; not every person who supports the pro-life agenda will be amicable toward refugees and asylum seekers. However, appealing to that sense of humanity is a great way to start a conversation.

ENGAGING THE SINGLE ISSUE VOTER MORE BROADLY

Single-issue voters can be easily manipulated. If all they care about or research is which candidate is pro-life, they will miss out on so many other policies that profoundly affect their communities. Single-issue voters are also less likely to engage in primaries because they might assume candidates in their party share the same belief on a specific issue, which isn't always true. They can fall prey to rhetoric that focuses on one issue or support an extreme candidate without fully realizing the repercussions of electing that person to office. When people take into consideration the whole policy package, they pick better leaders who will be more responsive to the community's needs. If a politician only needs to say they are anti-gun to win your vote, they are less incentivized to follow through on other issues. We can hold politicians accountable when we pick them based on the summation of their ideals, not just a single point.

My hope is you encourage the single-issue voters in your life to not just stare at the sand looking for one shell, like I used to do on the beach in the summer, but instead to take moments to assess other policies and influences on their political sphere. Today, I still walk the shoreline looking for shells, but I take moments to enjoy the cool breeze, look out on the horizon, and watch for footballs.

CHAPTER 12

THE NEW VOTER

Clipboard cadets are what I call the Greenpeace, Amnesty International, and DARE program representatives. They are people who have a high tolerance for being ignored by their fellow citizens and, I suspect, enjoy bothering strangers. I hate being approached by these well-meaning members of society. It's not because I don't agree with their work or am a sour person; I'm usually quite friendly. But do I want to talk to a stranger trying to get me to give them money on a Tuesday afternoon? Absolutely not.

There is one breed of clipboard cadet that my instincts didn't tell me to run from—the ones registering people to vote. I liked them because the moment you said, "I'm already registered," they would cheer or give you a high five, and you could be on your merry way guilt-free.

What if instead of just sniping college students leaving the library, these voter registration volunteers took their battle to the American high school? Most people are eighteen in their senior year of high school. I was seventeen, and trust me, being the youngest in your grade is annoying. Think about how excited everyone was when they were first able to drive, and everyone would show off their driver's license and post cringe photos with car keys? What if we could harness that FOMO phenomenon but with voting? I want Instagram feeds filled with high school seniors posting extremely vain pictures with the caption, "Just registered to vote #democracy." That is a cringe I can support. The truth is, we don't do enough to help new voters get started. And since we have this gift of the right to vote, we should make sure everyone gets it on their eighteenth birthday.

New voters aren't just eighteen year olds; citizens can be new voters at any age. Results from the Census Bureau's Current Population Survey give insight into who exactly these new voters were in the 2020 election. Overall voter turnout was 66.8 percent in 2020, "the biggest turnout in a presidential election since 1992 (67.7 percent) and more than five points higher than the 2016 election." There were six points or greater increases compared to 2016 from Latino, Asian American, and non-college white voters. Over half of those between ages eighteen and twenty-nine turned up on Election Day, up eight points from 2016. We see new voters in virtually every category, but why didn't these people participate in earlier elections? And how do we reach more Americans?

There is no singular type of new voter, and no number of categories could cover the nuance of every American's individual story. Instead, I want to dive into some of the experiences potential new voters face and what we can learn from them.

"MY PARENTS DIDN'T VOTE."

It wasn't until the Voting Rights Act of 1965 that black people in this country truly were able to vote. Some people alive today did not have the right to vote on their eighteenth birthday like the rest of us. If your parents went to college, you're highly likely to go to college, and if they didn't, chances are you won't either. The same can be true for voting. If you didn't grow up watching your parents vote, you might not have thought it mattered or was necessary. I spoke with a young black man named Adrian from Louisiana. He told me, "My parents don't vote. I don't think they have ever even registered. I didn't start voting until a girl I was dating, who was very into politics and activism, made me register. I guess I just didn't really think about it." His girlfriend was also raised in Louisiana, but her family was all about the right to vote. They have a scrapbook from the sixties with pictures of her grandparents voting for the first time. Adrian laughed when he told me he and the girl who made him a voter broke up a while ago: "She got me good because I can never go to the ballot box without thinking about her. I vote every time because I know my vote matters, but wow, she lives rent-free in my head to this day!" Adrian isn't the only one with parents who didn't vote.

A young woman I interviewed didn't grow up with an example of voting because her mom is undocumented. She remarked, "Because my mom is undocumented and there's not really a path to citizenship for her, I grew up wary of the government and putting my name on forms, even though I am fully a US citizen. I always worried it would get traced back to my mom somehow." Once she moved away from home, she began voting and registered the rest of her family, who are all legal US citizens. Many children of immigrants, legal or undocumented, have not grown up with an example of voting. Instead, they have to forge that path on their own. Of course, they will find lots of clipboard cadets chasing them down on college campuses. But if they don't go to college or become citizens post-college, there are fewer opportunities to jumpstart their voter registration. People whose parents weren't or aren't voters are enormous benefactors of community voter registration drives. Think back to the movement Stacey Abrams started in Georgia that registered hundreds of thousands of people. Of course, not all of them had non-voting parents, but it's safe to say many of them came from that situation. Furthermore, Adrian's story highlights how even just making sure everyone in your social circle is a voter can make a significant impact.

"I'M NEW HERE, LITERALLY."

As detailed by Nolo Press, "Once you have taken the oath of allegiance, have your naturalization certificate, and are officially a US citizen, you may register to vote in all federal, state, and local elections." According to the Department of Homeland Security, in 2019, 843,593 naturalizations occurred in the United States; that's almost a million new voters. Some states, like California, have information readily available to new citizens on how to register either online or through physical paperwork. In Los Angeles, "the community and voter outreach team routinely attends naturalization ceremonies in Los Angeles County to register new citizens to vote. At each ceremony, anywhere from 900 to 5,000 applicants are registered and offered an opportunity to register to vote. In 2012, the LA County Registrar found that nearly 30,000 new citizens registered to vote at naturalization ceremonies." There will be some naturalized citizens who are highly educated and informed of their rights and excited to exercise them, and others who might be so focused on naturalization, the right to vote is on the backburner.

Anuj Gurung is one of the former. He came from Kathmandu, Nepal, to the United States for college back in 2004 and since then has earned a Master's degree from Georgetown University and a PhD at Kent State. Now married to a woman from Ohio, he has finally decided to become a US citizen. He sees America as his home and while it's much easier to travel on an American passport, he is most enthusiastic about the opportunity to vote. Gurung told the New Americans Campaign, "My wife always says that she wants me to get citizenship because I am more informed than a lot of people who vote. I consider myself very informed politically. I teach political science conflict resolution courses. So it is frustrating that my participation in civics and politics is not a direct one. All I can do is talk about it. It would be a privilege to be able to participate directly in the democratic process of the United States of America." Gurung submitted his application for citizenship almost a year ago and, if bureaucracy runs smoothly, could be voting in the 2022 midterm elections.

A few years back, I worked with refugees teaching English classes and assisting in their case management at a nonprofit in Boston. These people were similar to Gurung. They were excited to be in America and full of hope for the American Dream. However, they did not wield three degrees and were more focused on putting food on the table than democratic participation. I recall asking a few of my clients from Sudan what they looked forward to the most in America. They were around the same age as me and shared the most ordinary things—finding a job, meeting someone special, and purchasing new shoes. We talked about citizenship, and each of them was excited by the prospect of truly being part of America, but voting never came up. At the end of my classes, I liked to share something about American culture or answer any questions they might have. I talked about baseball, Thanksgiving, why our hamburgers were so big, getting a driver's license, but never voting. Looking back, I should have, because democratic participation, while not uniquely American, is one of the many things that separates our country of opportunity from the poverty these refugees fled.

We need to be more cognizant of our new and future citizens. Whether it is a co-worker on a green card who was finally naturalized or a refugee sitting in your office, we need to talk about voting and share how to participate in our great democracy. More cities need to have voter registration available at naturalization ceremonies, and the citizenship process needs to include information on the importance of exercising your right to vote. Our democracy is stronger when more citizens vote.

THE NON-VOTER (HOPEFULLY) TURNED VOTER

This group is very tricky and not necessarily mutually exclusive from the other categories. In 2020, 67 percent of eligible voters cast a ballot, leaving eighty million people at home. NPR and the Medill School of Journalism commissioned Ipsos to survey adults who chose not to vote. They found that non-voters' reasons for not voting included: not being registered to vote (29 percent), not being interested in politics (23 percent), not liking the candidates (20 percent), feeling their vote wouldn't have made a difference (16 percent), and being undecided on whom to vote for (10 percent). The registration barrier can be combated by registration drives like those we discussed organized by Stacey Abrams in Georgia, the work of the League of Women Voters, and even just everyday people checking to see if members of their social circle are registered to vote.

Plenty of people aren't interested in politics. Plenty don't have time to research candidates. Plenty don't think their votes matter. That's the reason I decided to write this book. My hope is that if you're reading this, you can understand how much your vote can affect your community and the country. Not liking the candidates and being undecided go hand in hand. George W. Bush revealed in a *People Magazine* interview that he wrote in Condoleezza Rice for the 2020 presidential election. So if someone who was president for two terms and a gem of the GOP couldn't pick who to vote for and didn't like his options, it makes perfect sense that plenty of everyday Americans would feel the same way. My response to that connects to what we will talk about in Chapter 14: How Politics Works. In short, local elections matter because those are the people who the parties train for state and national elections. The best way to have candidates you like in big elections is to vote for those you love in the small ones.

I genuinely believe that the eighty million people who were eligible to vote in 2020 but chose not to would have been voters if, somewhere along the line, someone had shown them the importance of voting. It could be as simple as registering to vote in high school and talking about the importance of participating in democracy in your social studies class. Registering to vote at eighteen needs to be commonplace. Twenty-nine percent of those who didn't vote in 2020 couldn't because they weren't registered. Let us invest in our youth and instill in them the privilege and responsibility of the vote. The National Center for Education Statistics reports that 86 percent of public high school students will graduate, meaning at least 86 percent of the newly eligible voters are reachable in high schools across the country.

HOW CAN YOU ENCOURAGE THEM TO TAKE PART IN DEMOCRACY?

As we have discussed, there are many reasons someone might not participate in elections. If their parents didn't vote, be compassionate as to why their parents didn't participate. Remember that their parents' voting status is not a reflection of them.

If they are new to the United States, be enthusiastic about participating in democracy. It is likely that wherever they came from, they might not have been afforded such rights or had a government that respects the electoral process. This conversation is an excellent opportunity to share a piece of what makes America great.

For any non-voter, remember to connect how voting can positively and negatively affect your shared community. We often think of voting in the big picture, such as how the president will shift national policy. However, a new voter is likely not wrapped up in those debates and instead might benefit from being shown how politicians and their policies directly affect their lives.

You have so much influence over your social circle. Wield it wisely.

PART 4

BUILDING A STRONGER POLITICAL MINDSET

CHAPTER 13

HOW POLITICS WORKS

I wish there were a "Schoolhouse Rock!" song for this. Did your teacher play the "I'm Just a Bill" music video in your social studies class? It is three minutes of pure excellence. Dave Frishberg's lyrics start, "I'm just a bill, yes, I'm only a bill, and I'm sitting here on Capitol Hill." It sings you through the steps of a bill becoming a law, from just being an idea, to the representative drafting legislation and introducing it to Congress, to sitting in committee, to congressional debates, to votes in the House and Senate, to waiting for the president's signature, and *ta-da*, the bill is a law. The song captures the processes of the presidential veto and the two-thirds override. It's highly educational.

In lieu of a musical performance we'll run through the various cogs that makeup the machine and answer the question: How does politics work?

THE LEVELS

There are three main levels of the political system: federal, state, and local.

Federal is everything contained in the three national branches; executive, judicial, and legislative. This level includes the president, his cabinet, Supreme Court justices, federal judges, the House of Representatives, and the Senate.

The state level includes the governor, lieutenant governor, State Senate, State House of Representatives, state judges, and other positions like railroad commissioner.

Local level is everything else from the city council to the mayor to the county sheriff.

The local and state levels are often considered political training grounds for each party because successful candidates from these levels will be put up for federal elections. For example, Beth Van Duyne was on the city council of Irving, Texas, and then became a successful mayor of Irving. She was then put up for election to represent Texas' Twenty-Fourth District in Congress and won. If she continues to be successful, she could run for Senate someday. Or look at Barack Obama; he was a senator for Illinois before he ran for president. Pete Buttigieg went from mayor of South Bend, Indiana, to the US Secretary of Transportation and the first openly gay cabinet member. It isn't often that someone comes out of the blue like Donald Trump to sweep in at the federal level. This is why these lower-level positions are so important; not only do they decide issues that directly affect your community, but this is also their training to make more significant decisions for your state and even the country down the line. You never know who from your hometown will jump to the national stage.

There is a joke in politics that everyone hates Ted Cruz. Former US Senator Al Franken famously wrote in his autobiography, "I like Ted Cruz more than most of my other colleagues like Ted Cruz. And I hate Ted Cruz." Former Speaker of the House John Boehner, a Republican from Ohio, called Cruz "Lucifer in the flesh" on *The Late Show with Stephen Colbert*, and in his book *On the House*, he shared,"[Cruz] didn't do anything in the Senate but make noise and come over to the House side and stir up some of my more conservative members . . . into doing things that made no sense whatsoever." You'll recall from Chapter 2 that Beto couldn't oust Ted Cruz. Even though Cruz is widely despised, even by his peers, he holds his position as a senator. To prevent politicians like Cruz from being re-elected, we have to seek out and raise new political leaders who can challenge his stronghold. One way to do that is through the primary.

THE PRIMARY

There are many different types of primary races, and different states use different formats.

Closed Primaries: This primary type is used in Delaware, Florida, Kentucky, Maryland, Nevada, New Mexico, New York, Oregon, and Pennsylvania. It is called closed because you can only vote in these primaries if you are a registered party member. For example, if you are a registered

Republican, you can vote in the Republican primary, but you cannot vote in either primary if you are independent.

Partially Closed Primaries: This is the same setup as a closed primary, but political parties can allow unaffiliated voters to participate in their primary. The parties can change their inclusion rules each election cycle, which can be confusing for unaffiliated voters. Oklahoma, Connecticut, Idaho, North Carolina, South Dakota, and Utah use this format.

Partially Open Primaries: Voters can cross party lines but must publicly declare their ballot choice, or their ballot selection may be regarded as a form of registration with the corresponding party. In Iowa, voters choose a party on the state voter registration form, but voters can change their party affiliation for primary elections. The partially open format is used in Illinois, Indiana, Iowa, Ohio, Tennessee, and Wyoming.

Open to Unaffiliated Voters: This system allows unaffiliated voters to participate in whatever primary they choose. However, affiliated voters (those registered with a party) have to vote in their party's primary. Arizona, Colorado, Kansas, Maine, Massachusetts, New Hampshire, New Jersey, Rhode Island, and West Virginia use this format.

Open Primaries: Voters can choose in private which primary they want to vote in; they don't have to register to vote with the party. This means voters can cross party lines, and a Republican can vote in the Democrat's primary and vice versa. Open primaries are used in Alabama, Arkansas, Georgia, Hawaii, Michigan, Minnesota, Mississippi, Missouri, Montana, North Dakota, South Carolina, Texas, Vermont, Virginia, and Wisconsin.

Top-Two Primaries: This type is only used in California and Washington. It uses a common ballot where all the primary contestants are on the same form regardless of party. The two candidates with the most votes advance to the general election. This means there can be a general election with two Republicans or two Democrats or one of each.

The remaining three states not listed, Louisiana, Nebraska, and Alaska, have their unique primary systems. Louisiana doesn't really have a primary. Instead, all candidates run on the same ticket on the general election day. If no candidate receives over 50 percent of the vote, the top two vote-getters move on to a run-off election six weeks later. Nebraska has candidates run without a listed party; all candidates are listed on the same nonpartisan primary ballot. While a candidate doesn't say, "Hey, I'm Republican," their policies can tell you which side of the spectrum they fit in best. Alaska uses an open primary system where the top four candidates advance to the general election.

Unfortunately, while these primary formats apply to state and congressional races, they don't necessarily remain the same for presidential elections. Alaska, Arizona, California, Connecticut, Hawaii, Kansas, Louisiana, Maine, Michigan, Nebraska, New Jersey, North Dakota, and Washington use different formats for the presidential primaries than they do for other races.

My home state uses the open primary format, so as an independent, I can participate in the primary of my choosing. I look at Louisiana's primary—or lack thereof—and can't help but think it would be much easier to get everyone to come out and vote on one day than to do this dance with primaries. However, the primary system was designed to give citizens more power in the selection of candidates.

INVENTING THE PRIMARY

Primaries were developed in the early twentieth century; previously, the caucus format was used to select candidates. While there are still caucuses today, they are less prevalent. Before primaries, it was challenging for new faces to break into the political scene. Candidates needed support from the party leadership, who acted as gatekeepers, only allowing passage for the elites and political insiders.

In the early 1900s, Wisconsin Governor Robert LaFollette was fed up with backroom politics and drafted legislation that allowed Wisconsin voters to have more say over convention delegate selection. This opened a floodgate for voters eager to seize control of fielding representatives. By 1916, twenty-five of the forty-eight states had presidential primaries and more solidified rules binding delegates to popular election results. 1960 was the year the power of the primary reared its head on the national level. Lyndon

B. Johnson (LBJ) was the favorite for the Democrats and, without primaries, would have been the nominee. However, John F. Kennedy won several Democratic primaries and became the nominee even though party leadership wanted LBJ. From this point forward, presidential nominations increasingly relied on the will of the people and their voice during the primaries. Primaries ensure that the general public—average party members or unaffiliated voters depending on the state—get to choose who runs in the general, not political elites. But it goes beyond making our representative democracy more egalitarian. It gives the people an opportunity to signal to the party what issues they feel strongly about.

PRIMARY POWER: THE SANDERS EFFECT

Bernie Sanders, the senator from Vermont, changed the landscape of the Democratic Party over his two presidential nominee runs. In 2016 he was the furthest-left candidate on almost every issue. He advocated for a 10 percent tax surcharge on billionaires, free college for all Americans, a single-payer government-run health insurance system, and lower prices on pharmaceuticals, and allowing Americans to import medications from Canada where they are less expensive. An article from Daniel Strauss in July 2016 opens, "Bernie Sanders has pushed Hillary Clinton so far to the left that she's poised to embrace a Democratic Party platform draft that's nothing short of radical," a commentary on a new wave of understanding on how Bernie Sanders has influenced the party. Sanders was able to drive Democrats to accept more liberal policies because he received such high voter support. He forced politicians like Hillary Clinton to jump in his lane in order to stay competitive.

His power for change was recognized on both sides of the aisle. The Republican aligned research organization America Rising Squared released a primer titled "The Sanders Manifesto," which states, "Bernie Sanders may have lost the Democrat Primary in 2016, but history will show he left an indelible mark on the Democrat Party for decades to come. His longer than expected presence in the race provided a vessel for the restless and upstart Elizabeth Warren wing and sent the party lurching leftward at a torrid pace. Over the weekend, the Democratic Party officially approved what Sanders proudly declared the most progressive platform in its history. The document lays out the new policies of the Democrats with the expressed purpose of providing an in-depth look at just how extreme the policies of 'the new Democratic Party' really are."

Since Hillary lost the 2016 election, Sanders' ideas were not implemented, and the country swung to the right. However, his influence was not a flash in the pan. In 2020 the ideas that felt radical just four years prior were embraced by other candidates in the Democratic primary. Most Democrats got on board with a form of tuition-free or debt-free college; five agreed with Sanders that college should be free, and six others thought two years should be free. Two candidates agreed with Sanders on Medicare for All; seven others wanted Medicare for All but would accept legislation that expanded Medicare. Nine candidates agreed with Sanders that would allow the government to break patents of brand drug companies to make cheaper generics available quicker and allowing drug importation from countries where costs are lower. Eight candidates agreed with Sanders that there should be special taxes on wealth, and four thought the US government should increase existing taxes on upper-income Americans. It is impressive how much the Democratic Party shifted on policy. Thanks to the outpour of voter support for the Vermont senator and constituent pressure on other candidates, Sanders' ideas were now mainstream.

Democrats across the country recognized Sanders's contribution, and he won primaries in New Hampshire, Nevada, California, Colorado, Utah, Vermont, and North Dakota. On April 8, 2020, Sanders drops out of the race, one of the last men standing out of a vast field but not the winner. Though Biden was the winner, there were around twenty more primaries to go. One would think people would either vote for Biden or not bother voting because it wouldn't change the outcome that Biden was going to the general election. However, many Democrats took this moment to make a point and signal they supported Sanders's further-left ideas, with the hope Biden would recognize their voice. After Sanders dropped out of the race, he received 135 more delegates. Bernie Sanders's ideas are now engrained in the Democratic Party's platform, despite never winning the presidential nomination. This case shows how primary elections can push a party to change its positions and bring new ideas into the fold. If the voting public hadn't come out in force in support of Sanders, these policies would never have left Vermont. Primaries can make change happen when citizens participate.

Republican primaries have been just as persuasive in shifting policy. Before Donald Trump won the Republican primary in 2016, it felt like the nominee would bring a return to Bush-era policies and scale back some Obama reforms. The faces included Ted Cruz, Marco Rubio, John Kasich, Ben Carson, and Jeb Bush. Trump was the furthest to the right of any of the candidates. While they mostly agreed on opposing new gun control laws, doubt of man-made climate change, and not allowing refugees, Trump was the only candidate to support deporting undocumented immigrants. President Trump was more of a symptom than a catalyst of this shift to the right. According to the General Social Survey, self-identified Republicans have consistently moved far more toward the highly conservative part of the scale over the past several decades. Republicans now in Congress are further to the right than those in office in the 1970s and 1980s.

Consider conservatives like House Speaker John Boehner, Ohio Governor John Kasich, and Senator John McCain. They were all strong conservatives during the Bush era but have found themselves categorized as moderates as time passed. Republicans had the opportunity to choose a moderate in their 2016 primary; John Kasich was in the race. There was also Marco Rubio, and though considering him a more moderate Republican is a stretch, he did vote to terminate President Trump's declaration of national emergency at the US-Mexico border in March 2019. The people didn't want Kasich or a nicely wrapped Rubio; they wanted Trump. In many ways, he represented what they had been feeling for years, and picking him in the primary was the way to make that undeniably known. Without Republicans making their voices heard in the 2016 primary, political elites might have put a third Bush in office.

Voting in the primary on any level of government is an opportunity to demonstrate to party leadership the direction of change you desire. Primaries are the moments where organizations like the Justice Democrats and Young Republicans National Federation can present candidates divergent from the norm. We wouldn't have Madison Cawthorn, AOC, or any of their colleagues without people showing up for the primary. Primaries put new faces and new ideas into the heart of our political system, and we must consistently participate in them.

INITIATIVES AND REFERENDUMS

While local and state systems prepare candidates for the federal level and primaries allow citizens to push their party along the political spectrum, there are times when we can't wait for the seeds we planted to grow. Lucky for us, our predecessors already came to that conclusion and put two systems in place, the initiative and referendum processes.

Initiative: This is defined by the National Conference of State Legislatures (NCSL) as "a process that enables citizens to bypass their state legislature by placing proposed statutes and constitutional amendments on the ballot in some states. A total of twenty-four states have the citizen initiative process." In the direct initiative process, citizens can collect a certain number of signatures to get their proposal placed on the ballot. People then either vote for or against the initiative. There is also an indirect process where signatures are still collected; however, it allows the state legislature to act on the proposal. If signatures were collected for buses to be required to stop at train tracks, the indirect system would allow the state legislature a chance to draft a law for this proposal. If the legislature decides not to take action, the initiative question goes on the ballot. Yet, the legislature can offer an alternative option on the ballot. If the people proposed buses must stop at train tracks, the legislature could propose that buses stop at train tracks when children are on board. Then the public votes on which initiative they prefer.

States with Citizen Initiatives: Alaska, Arizona, Arkansas, California, Colorado, Florida, Idaho, Illinois, Maine, Massachusetts, Michigan, Mississippi, Missouri, Montana, Nebraska, Nevada, North Dakota, Ohio, Oklahoma, Oregon, South Dakota, Utah, Washington, Wyoming

Referendum: NCSL writes, "The popular referendum is a device which allows voters to approve or repeal an act of the legislature. If the legislature passes a law that voters do not approve of, voters may gather signatures to demand a popular vote on the law." This method also requires a collection of signatures. Once the movement has enough signatures, the new law will be placed on the ballot, and the people will have the opportunity to vote on it. If the law is approved, it will take effect, and if not, it will be voided entirely.

States with Popular Referendums: Alaska, Arizona, Arkansas, California, Colorado, Idaho, Maine, Maryland, Massachusetts, Michigan, Missouri, Montana, Nebraska, Nevada, New Mexico, North Dakota, Ohio, Oklahoma, Oregon, South Dakota, Utah, Washington, Wyoming

As someone from a state with neither citizen initiatives nor popular referendums, I implore you to wisely wield this gift. In 2014, Alaska, Arkansas, Illinois, Nebraska, and South Dakota all had referendums to increase the minimum wage. The vote resulted in all five states increasing worker wages, a massive demonstration of the power of referendums. Marijuana legalization often happens through citizen initiatives and referendums. Five states (Vermont, Illinois, New Mexico, New York, Virginia) legalized the substance through legislative bills. In comparison, twelve states did so through ballot measures (Alaska, Arizona, California, Colorado, Maine, Massachusetts, Michigan, Montana, Nevada, New Jersey, Oregon, Washington).

Referendums and initiatives are opportunities for pure democracy rather than representative democracy and should not be squandered. They aren't always on politically touchy topics like minimum wage or marijuana legalization; they can be particular to the state. Maine had a referendum in 2014 about bears. The question was, "Do you want to ban the use of bait, dogs, or traps in bear hunting except to protect property, public safety, or for research?" Mainers said no. So if you're a bear and somehow reading this, do not go to Maine for vacation. Presque Isle is a beautiful place, but they might try and kill you, using old donuts as bait. In all seriousness, these ballot measures are a powerful tool. With enough signatures, you can put anything on the ballot.

THE RECALL

Signatures go a long way in terms of increasing political agency. Aside from citizen initiatives and referendums, they can be used to recall state officials. NCSL defines a recall as "a procedure that allows citizens to remove and replace a public official before the official's term of office ends." Nineteen states and the District of Columbia allow for recalls of state officials (Alaska, Arizona, California, Colorado, Georgia, Idaho, Illinois, Kansas, Louisiana, Michigan, Minnesota, Montana, Nevada, New Jersey, North Dakota, Oregon, Rhode Island, Washington, Wisconsin). A recall is different from impeachment. Whereas impeachment is a legal process that requires specific charges, recalls in most states don't require specific grounds. If you don't like how the official performs their job and you can get enough signatures of people who agree with you, you can have a recall.

A recall is a check on the power of officials. Many politicians make promises on the campaign trail that they don't deliver on once in office, but knowing that if they deviate too heavily from the mandate that put them in office could wind them up in a recall is pressure for them to stay the course. In 2003, California held a recall election of Governor Gray Davis, just eleven months after he was elected. The cause for recall was a combination of factors; the moment in history was politically difficult with the dot-com collapse, stalled economy, and budget deficit of thirty-eight billion dollars. *The New York Times* said the "underlying reason for his ruin . . . was a failing of political character: He was, essentially, a loner. He did not talk to voters. He did not talk to legislators. . . . He got his start in politics behind the scenes, and that was where he was comfortable. Californians made their disapproval known and successfully recalled Gray Davis on October 7, 2003. The newly elected governor was none other than Arnold Schwarzenegger himself.

Recall elections aren't as rare as one might presume. "2011, the Year of the Recall" was the title of a piece by Joshua Spivak that published in December of that year. He cites 150 officials in seventeen states that faced recall votes, including thirty mayors. The contagion of recalls in 2011 is due, in part, to people realizing their agency and being able to connect with others more easily through social media, Instagram launched in October 2010. Increased connection via the internet meant that people in Rhode Island could see in near-real time how people in North Dakota executed a recall. If they can, why not us? More recently, California Governor Gavin Newsom faced a recall election that drew national attention, but the effort was defeated and Newsom won by a 27 percent margin. Recalls don't always achieve their intended outcome, but they bring scrutiny to the reasons the effort came about in the first place; and when they do succeed they facilitate big change.

Politics is complicated.

The primary process is the gatekeeper of the general election; its job is to ensure that whoever is selected to represent the party truly embodies the people's will. In a two-party system with a breadth of ideas under a single umbrella, people must participate in their primaries. It is the difference between sending a far-right politician or a Bush-era Republican to the general—the difference between a leftist and a liberal. You get to choose.

Through special maneuvers, the Terminator becomes governor, and weed is legalized in some states. If your community is passionate about something, check out your state's rules on referendums and citizen initiatives, or the next time an organizer asks for your signature, be armed with the knowledge of what that signature can do.

Take local elections seriously. The local level is the farm team, the training camp for politicians to potentially rise to national stardom. Whoever excels at the local level builds a base to move up to the state and even national levels. The politicians that represent you in the most prominent offices in the nation started somewhere. Joe Biden was a New Castle County council member before being elected to the Senate. George H. W. Bush was in the House of Representatives for Texas' Seventh District.

Never forget that you, the individual, the informed citizen, have the power to make politics work for your community.

CHAPTER 14

CREATING TRANSPARENCY

Have you ever walked out the front door and asked yourself whether you turned off the oven? You run back in, of course, because on the off chance you didn't, it would nag at you all day. My dance team would always do dress checks before we loaded the bus for a competition. We had to take out every item of every costume and show it to the coach to prove we didn't leave anything at home. It was an annoying task for four in the morning, taking out the tan jazz shoes and the blue scrunchies, the tan tights, and the red lipstick. But it saved us from that nagging feeling we had forgotten something and the wrath of our coach if we had indeed misplaced a costume piece. When you vote, there's no good way to check if your team—your neighbors, your social circle, have also returned their ballots. You can ask around, and that's encouraged, but I wished there was a systematic way to see what communities weren't voting. If we know who isn't voting, then we know where to focus our engagement efforts. Just like if you know that one teammate that always forgets her tights, you can remind them. So much happens during the voting season; it's easy for someone to forget, just like you might have forgotten to turn off the stove last night. Lucky for us, there's a group of people who have come up with a solution.

The Center for Inclusive Democracy at the USC Sol Price School of Public Policy does undeniably innovative work, a model for the future of tracking voting in this country. The Center for Inclusive Democracy or CID "conducts a range of national and multi-state research initiatives exploring voting behavior, civic engagement, electoral and economic research, the intersection of social justice and democracy, and more." They believe "inclusive civic and political participation is critical in addressing disparities in social and economic well-being, and can improve health, education, and employment outcomes."

I had the honor of speaking with CID's founder and director, Professor Mindy Romero. She explained her motivation for starting CID: "It was just something that I felt compelled to do; that there was this need, this unmet need, in terms of a center that was really focused on producing research that was accessible and digestible, to the public to policymakers to advocacy groups, community groups, and had a lens that was going to be woven through every research question, which is what does this mean in terms of disparities as much as this mean in terms of equity and representation."

They have developed two cutting edge tools to assist voters and promote democratic participation without infringing on civil liberties. Professor Romero affirmed their commitment to privacy, sharing, "Everything we use is publicly available already and we don't present any individual data."

The two tools are the voting location siting tool and the ballot return tool. These aren't available in every part of the United States yet, but CID is actively expanding and perfecting their models.

VOTING LOCATION SITING TOOL

According to CID's website this tool "uses a web-based interactive data mapping system to identify areas within a half-mile in diameter where vote centers and polling places would likely have the most success in serving voters, especially harder-to-reach underserved voting populations. The technology identifies areas through a facility allocation model that incorporates local demographic and historical voting data, which the user can then customize based on specific local needs." The tool tells election officials the best places to put polling locations so that everyone in the community can have equal access to the ballot. In the 2020 election, Texas mandated that each county only have one ballot drop box. This type of setup isn't too bad if you live in the panhandle, but in Harris County, which includes Houston, that's 4.7 million people for one ballot box. Now, if Texas had used the voting location sitting tool, this wouldn't have happened. Shamefully, the instrument was available for Texas in the 2020 election, but I guess Governor Greg Abbot didn't get the memo. Harris County ended up using the siting tool for their in-person voting, but because the one county one box mandate was upheld by Texas courts, their hands were tied when it came to ballot drop-off. Speaking of the tool, Benjamin Chou, special assistant and director of innovation office of the Harris County Clerk, said in a testimonial, "We in Harris County much enjoyed working with the Center for Inclusive Democracy and highly recommend the siting tool to others!"

The tool was first launched during the 2018 California primary election cycle and is now available in ten states: Arizona, California, Colorado, Florida, Georgia, Michigan, North Carolina, Pennsylvania, Texas, and Wisconsin. This means that 43 percent of the US population has access to this technology. The parts of the country that have utilized this tool have had great success. Judd Choate, state election director from the Colorado Secretary of State's office, shared, "The Colorado Voter Service and Polling Center (VSPC) siting tool is a fantastic source of important historical and demographic information so that counties can select the best possible VSPC locations, and the public can better understand these selections. Mindy Romero's team worked tirelessly to update the tool to fit Colorado's specific needs. We have already identified ways to make the VSPC siting tool even better in the next iteration."

I decided to put the tool to the test myself. One of the great things about the Center for Inclusive Democracy is that their technology is publicly accessible, meaning citizens can hold their representatives to account if they don't place voting locations in an equitable data-driven manner. I went to their website, clicked the voting location siting tool, and then on the map clicked Texas. It opens a map of Texas and shows the counties where they have data (as of this writing, they only have the most populated counties but have plans to expand to the entire state). Dallas County is where I grew up and where my parents still reside. Once I selected Dallas County, it showed a zoomed-in map of the area and multiple options for vote center areas. It had 463 suggested areas for Election Day Vote Centers, sixty recommended areas for early vote centers, 2,138 potential areas, and forty-seven additional vote-center options based on their model. Trying to keep it simple, I looked into the suggested areas for early vote centers. Using the map, I could find my neighborhood, and CID suggested the closest early voting center. I am somewhat pleased with whoever is the elections director for our area because the actual early voting location isn't too far off from what CID suggested.

But it doesn't stop here, CID also provides demographic and voter data, including percent of county voting-age citizens, percent of county workers, percent of eligible voters not registered, percent of the population with vehicle access, percent of the population in poverty, population density (per square kilometer), 2020 polling place voter percentage, 2020 vote by mail rate (total), 2020 vote by mail rate (Asian American), 2020 vote by mail rate (Latino), 2020 vote by mail rate (youth). You can select these markers and see a map of the county color-coded according to the percentages. For the total 2020 vote by mail rate, I can see which parts of Dallas County had a 12 percent or higher vote by mail rate and the areas where less than 5.2 percent voted by mail. In my neighborhood, between 7.1 and 9.0 percent of voters used vote by mail. It is exciting to have so much data organized in one place. Election officials and volunteer organizations can use these numbers to help improve our existing election system so it is secure and equitable.

BALLOT RETURN TOOL

CID defines this tool as "a first-of-its-kind, data-driven interactive mapping resource for visualizing early ballots cast in real-time by registered voters during an election, whether the voting happens in person or by mail." The tool uses publicly available data and is not mining anything private. It only tracks early ballots cast by registered voters on the county or precinct level and updates the data in real-time. This means a group of volunteers can get together at 5:30 on a Tuesday and see where in their area people have already cast ballots. Then they can organize their outreach activities to those zones where less voting has occurred. The beauty of this tool is that it helps community organizers and non-profit organizations maximize the impact of their outreach by showing what areas need the most encouragement to participate.

Officials first used the tool in Los Angeles County for the 2020 General Election. It was then implemented in Georgia to "assist election officials and community groups there involved in voter outreach for the January 2021 US Senate runoff elections." I used the tool to zoom into the exact precinct where I lived for a few years while attending USC. The precinct is a couple of blocks, a tiny and specific area. There were 142 registered voters in this zone for 2020, and they cast seventy-two total votes, meaning 50.7 percent of total registered voters cast ballots, significantly below the Los Angeles County average of 75.5 percent registered voters casting ballots. My former precinct would have been a strong candidate for more voter outreach and messaging. This tool can help community organizers streamline their work and support organizations like the League of Women Voters to track their impact in real-time. If you have a meeting or email blast or go door to door in a neighborhood and then see that those precincts had an increase in ballot return rate, you know your message worked, and if not, you know to go back to the drawing board. I could see if my neighborhood is participating in democracy and know if I need to step up my game in talking about our right to vote.

THE NEXT ELECTION

CID has already committed to expanding their tools to Ohio, Virginia, Hawaii, and Nevada. Professor Romero shared they are "establishing connections, trying to get a lot of input on the tool to see where it's appropriate for us to customize a little bit more to the unique needs of each state." She presents to election officials at state and national conferences, detailing their methodology and goals. Through these presentations, as well as direct outreach, CID encourages election officials to utilize their free tools. Naturally, officials have a healthy level of skepticism when it comes to the voting system they have been assigned to protect. However, CID's nonpartisan, non-advocacy, purely research-based structure allows them to build relationships with a variety of stakeholders, especially election officials. CID's work is for democracy, not a particular party or group or subset of Americans; it is data for everyone.

Looking ahead, Professor Romero is focused on building the trust CID has established in many states across the country. She shared, "[We're] being clear and careful and purposeful in the outreach so people understand where we're coming from. . . . Data is empowering. It always has been data-driven solutions that are important, but I think now they are more than ever. Having transparent data tools everyone can understand and use are critical to building trust. Especially when we're in a world where many people have distrust of their election officials or the administration of elections. When you have some transparent tools that are available, I think that goes a long way. It's not the only thing you need right to build trust, but it can help out tremendously. And so I think any sort of data driven tools from nonpartisan sources should be embraced."

One of my final questions for Professor Romero was "Why do you vote?" Her life's work has been dedicated to voting accessibility, equity, and transparency for others, but what brings her to the ballot box election after election? She shared, "I vote because I connect voting to change and fairness and distribution of resources and life chances and community. As a kid, it was obvious the elected officials in my community were not serving everyone, I quickly realized that the communities that were being neglected had much lower [voter] turnout rates. It's not the only factor, but historically there's a direct relationship between low [voter] turnout and neglected communities in terms of access and distribution of resources."

Professor Romero is right: There is power in voting and trust in transparency.

The Center for Inclusive Democracy does not get nearly enough press coverage for the ground-breaking work they are doing. In a world where massive amounts of data are floating around, it would be remiss not to harness the information to further promote democratic participation. Supplied with the information of what locations would be most equitable and accessible for different neighbor-hoods and communities, we can ensure our system is not skewed against historically underserved areas and protect our democracy.

GO VOTE

I believe in a version of American exceptionalism.

My version is rooted in one central theme: The United States undertakes every challenge with a recognizable fervor, and even if everything comes crashing down, we remain proud to be American. Call it whatever you want—arrogant, nationalist, whatever. But you can't deny that it's true.

The history of the United States is the story of the battle for an equitable democracy. It is a march toward an ever-more-majestic American dream. Empires fallen, wars won, rights secured, and after almost 250 years of forward momentum, everyone can cast their ballot on Election Day regardless of race, sexuality, gender, ethnicity, or creed.

Democracy has never been perfect. But ignoring it—not taking advantage of your right to vote—spits on the sacrifices of those Americans who gave their lives in defense of the democratic process. Americans have fought for a better life from the moment the first settlers set foot in Jamestown, from the Nineteenth Amendment to the Civil Rights Movement, to the pushback on new laws that aim to restrict voting. Somewhere along that fight, we started to take voting for granted.

I hope that in knowing how hard it was to come this far, we reject complacency and protect our rights.

We are exceptional because:

- People like Beto O'Rourke can challenge the status quo, even in parts of this country that run the deepest red or the bluest blue. No matter where you are, when you organize, you can force people to listen.
- Young Americans like Madison Cawthorn or Alexandria Ocasio-Cortez can be elected to Congress. In our country, you're never too young or too different to have an impact on your community.
- When constituents felt they weren't well represented, organizations like the Justice Democrats and Young Republicans National Federation stepped in to put new faces on the ballot. Strong women like Lauren Boebert and Ilhan Omar—they couldn't be more different but still represent what it means to be American.

You are part of this exceptionalism.

Think about the next election. You start seeing ads in the local media and signs going up in your neighbors' lawns. What do you do?

A great first step would be to use vote411.org to check your voter registration and then read about what items are on the ballot. Maybe this election cycle your district's House of Representatives seat is up for grabs and your mayor is running. It might sound a little too on the nose that a local politician is running for a seat in federal government, but this isn't a hypothetical example. This is the exact situation I found myself in for the 2020 election cycle. The mayor of my hometown, Beth Van Duyne, was running to represent the Twenty-Fourth District of Texas in the House.

Americans voted for several things in 2020, including the highest office in the land. As a firm believer in soft power and diplomacy, choosing a presidential candidate to support was easy. The rest of what would be on my ballot required a bit more legwork.

Voting consistently is crucial and voting in the primary is how you can ensure your personal brand of Democrat or Republican makes it to the general election. The primary took place on March 3, 2020. Texas has an open primary structure, meaning anyone can choose to vote in any primary; they don't have to be registered with that party. Anyone can change which primary they vote in with each new year if they so choose. The decision is usually easy for lifelong Democrats and Republicans; as an Independent, I had a choice to make. To help me decide which primary I wanted to vote in, I went to the League of Women Voters of Texas website. They had bios of each candidate and what their positions were on major issues. My mayor, Beth Van Duyne, was running as a Republican and facing a field of four other candidates. The Democrats had Candace Valenzuela from the Carollton-Farmers Branch School Board and six other candidates.

While everyone should make their own individual informed decision about who they vote for, it's impossible to completely block out all outside influence. You can see it in advertisements, bumper stickers, T-shirts, and more. Most of the signs in my neighborhood were for Beth Van Duyne, more than any of the other Republican candidates. Beth prevailed in the Republican primary. The Democratic primary went to a runoff, but Candace Valenzuela won in the end. It was Beth versus Candace in November.

Summer came and the world was upside down in new ways each week; we were socially distant but, in many aspects, forced closer to confronting our shortcomings. I spent time checking in with my friends and, of course, making sure they were registered to vote. When I talked to my fellow Texans, the younger conservatives said they enjoyed Beth's moderate approach to climate change and saw her as a pro-women figure; meanwhile, older conservatives were more focused on immigration and trade policy. On the other hand, local Democrats gravitated toward Candace's clear progressive policies and emphasis on education. The funny thing about local politics is that people in your social circle often have personal stories about the candidates. Part of my childhood was spent on a playground that Beth Van Duyne built through local donations, and Candace served the school district where I attended elementary and middle school. I admired both women. Beth was a single mom who had met with Israel's

Prime Minister Benjamin Netanyahu to discuss trade and traveled to Saudi Arabia to secure major investments for our area—all while being Mayor of a little city outside Dallas. Candace was emblematic of the American Dream: her family was once homeless, but she graduated high school with a full-ride to college and rooted her public service work in access to education for everyone.

In the end I decided to vote for the person who I thought would represent interests of the entire community in the Twenty-Fourth District and had a voice that aligned most closely with my priorities.

Election night was a roller coaster across the country, but the Twenty-Fourth District of Texas had its own loops. Beth Van Duyne claimed victory before the votes had been tallied and Candace Valenzuela's team refused to concede until the count was over. The end result gave Beth victory, but only by about five thousand votes. That's 0.6 percent of the population. Clearly the district was more purple than my conservative neighborhood might have led one to believe. Separate from the outcome, I was excited our district was finally competitive. It meant that now more than ever, every vote counts. If 0.6 percent of the population had voted differently or chosen to not vote at all, an entirely different person would be representing our district. Do I think 5,000 more Democratic votes were out there? Absolutely. And those people should be kicking themselves for not voting. Of course, I'm sure there were plenty of Republicans who sat it out as well, assuming a Beth victory. After seeing those margins, I doubt they'll make that mistake again. Every vote is essential to the American democratic experiment.

When's your next election? Who will you choose to represent you? Where do you stand on the issues? Use vote411.org for your voter information needs and be prepared to make a difference. Whether it's for mayor or president, your vote counts. Don't waste this opportunity to better your slice of America.

Go out and vote. Vote consistently. Vote often. Vote for yourself. Vote for your family's future. Vote for your community. Vote for your business. Vote because it is your right as an American.

God bless America. And God bless the American voter.

ACKNOWLEDGMENTS

I have wanted to write a book since I learned to read. In the first grade, I attempted to write one, an incoherent mess scribbled on pages of extra-wide ruled loose-leaf paper. Decades later, this book started out the same way, an incoherent mess written on a stray piece of printer paper. What those sentence fragments developed into would not have been possible without the people who supported me throughout this process.

First, I'd like to thank my family, who accepted that most conversations would devolve into a discussion of the American voter, reminded me of the importance of fresh eyes when I hit a roadblock, and provided encouragement when I needed it most.

Thank you to Christine Thielman, the first person outside of New Degree Press to see my manuscript. Her feedback and insights helped me angle my book for its intended audience.

My utmost appreciation to my dear friend Lauren Oberreiter, who pre-ordered my book within seconds of the link going live and always believes in my ventures.

I'm grateful for Melody Brown-Clark, who, upon me telling her I was writing a book, simply said, "That makes sense," even though in the beginning nothing about this made sense.

For the entire team at New Degree Press who patiently helped me navigate the publishing process as a first-time author. My developmental editor, Avery Lockland, for providing a non-judgmental sounding board for my most outlandish ideas and humorous takes on the differences between the US and Canada. My editor, Colin Lyon, for the countless Zoom calls and Quip pings. I deeply appreciate your ability to make sense of my babbling questions and understand exactly what I meant when I asked, "How do I un-weird this?"

Special thanks to Professor Eric Koester who called me in December 2020 and kickstarted this entire journey. His wisdom and unwavering support made this entire operation possible. Thank you for taking a chance on a new author on the other side of the country.

For Dr. Ann Crigler, Professor Mindy Romero, Sarah Courtney, and Jeanette Senecal. Their expertise allowed me to iron out the trickiest topics.

Thank you to all of the proud Americans who shared their stories with me. Your openness and honesty painted narratives that brought this book to life.

And of course, thank you to my early supporters: Joy Atkins, Lauren Bain, Alex Bosch, Lauren Bouvier, Melody Brown-Clark, Kristyn Byrd, Michael Byrne, Andrea Dawson, Jonathan Dawson, Jeana Dickinson, Jean-Paul Dubos, William Eithier, Alexandra Ecker, Allison Fasano, Jesus Fernandez, Steven Galloway, Keith Gannett, Mary Guzman, Elizabeth Hannan, Alex Horton, Pann Hmwe, John E. Kane, Dana Kelman, Jong Su (Yuma) Kim, Thomas Kim, Liz Kimball, Brady Lewis, Liv Liska, Sean Liew, Jacob Lokshin, Ryan Mackey, Kaluani Mambwe, Abby Merz, Ed Meziere, Mark Walter Mitchell, Nieves R Moya Jr, Kyle Mullenix, Tamara Newbre, Dr. Davy Norris, Lauren Oberreiter, Kim Ortiz, Brit Proctor, Jack Provost, Amy Ecker Ramirez, Wendy Reilly, Avis Robin, Lisa Russel, Debralynn Santora, Martin Santora, Joey Schewee, Nick Schiele, Anthony (Tony) Sinclair, Lisa Spraggins, Camille Stafford, Elizabeth Stevens, Gregory Thielman, Jeff Thielman, Lisa Thielman, Noah Thielman, Lisa Van Acker, Threcia Walls, Ethan Ward, and Craig Wexler.

APPENDIX

CHAPTER 1

"#Protect2020." *Cybersecurity and Infrastructure Security Agency CISA*. Accessed September 29, 2021. *https://www.cisa.gov/ protect2020*.

BUSH v GORE (Florida Supreme Court December 12, 2000). *https://www.law.cornell.edu/supct/html/00-949.ZPC.html*.

Childress, Sarah. "Court: North Carolina Voter ID Law Targeted Black Voters." PBS. Public Broadcasting Service. Accessed September 29, 2021. *https://www.pbs.org/wgbh/frontline/article/court-north-carolina-voter-id-law-targeted-black-voters/*.

Gore Al, "Al Gore Concedes the 2000 Election" November 7, 2000 The history place—great speeches Collection: Al Gore concedes the 2000 election, transcript and audio *https://www.historyplace.com/speeches/gore-concedes.htm*.

Posner, Mark A. and Lee Rowland. "RE: Comment Under Section 5, Submission No. 2011-2187." Brennan Center Files, Accessed September 29, 2021. *https://www.brennancenter.org/sites/*

*default/files/legacy/Democracy/VRE/Florida%20Section%20
5%20comment%20letter%20-%20FINAL.pdf.*

Pruitt, Sarah. "8 Most Contentious US Presidential Elections."
History.com. A&E Television Networks, April 26, 2016.
*https://www.history.com/news/most-contentious-u-s-presi-
dential-elections.*

"Shelby County v. Holder." Oyez , n.d. *https://www.oyez.org/
cases/2012/12-96.*

Solomon, Danyelle, et al. "Systematic Inequality and American
Democracy." Center for American Progress, Accessed September 29, 2021. *https://www.americanprogress.org/issues/
race/reports/2019/08/07/473003/systematic-inequality-amer-
ican-democracy/.*

"Standing Committee on Election Law—Current Litigation."
americanbar.org, n.d. *https://www.americanbar.org/groups/
public_interest/election_law/litigation/.*

CHAPTER 2

Anonymous Author. "Beto O'Rourke Raises $10.4 Million in Sec-
ond QUARTER, Doubling Ted Cruz's Numbers." FOX 4 News
Dallas-Fort Worth. FOX 4 News Dallas-Fort Worth, July 12,
2018. *https://www.fox4news.com/news/beto-orourke-raises-
10-4-million-in-second-quarter-doubling-ted-cruzs-numbers.*

Anonymous Author. "Beto O'Rourke on NFL Players Kneeling
During the National Anthem." Facebook. Accessed September 29, 2021. *https://www.facebook.com/NowThisPolitics/*

videos/beto-orourke-on-nfl-players-kneeling-during-the-na-
tional-anthem/2422498247760393/?extid=SEO——.

"Congressional District 2, Tx." Data USA. Accessed September 29, 2021. *https://datausa.io/profile/geo/congressional-district-2-tx.*

"Elizabeth Markowitz Election Results." Ballotpedia. Accessed September 29, 2021. *https://ballotpedia.org/Elizabeth_Markowitz.*

Goldsberry, Kirk. "What Really Happened In Texas." *FiveThirtyEight,* November 14, 2018. *https://fivethirtyeight.com/features/how-beto-orourke-shifted-the-map-in-texas/.*

House Archivists. "O'ROURKE, Beto." US House of Representatives: History, Art & Archives. Accessed September 29, 2021. *https://history.house.gov/People/Listing/O/O-ROURKE,-Beto-(O000170)/.*

Jones, Aria. "Watch: Houston-Area Congressional Candidate Sima LADJEVARDIAN Says District Dynamics Have 'Completely Changed.'" *The Texas Tribune,* September 29, 2020. *https://www.texastribune.org/2020/09/29/sima-ladjevardian-event/.*

Law, Tara. "Beto O'Rourke Says 'Hell Yes' He Wants to Take YOUR AR-15." *Time,* April 30, 2021. *https://time.com/5676620/beto-orourke-take-guns-ar15-ak47/.*

Lovegrove, Jamie. "Beto O'Rourke Launches 2018 Senate Campaign in Underdog Bid to Unseat Ted Cruz." *Dallas News,* March 31, 2017. *https://www.dallasnews.com/news/poli-*

tics/2017/03/31/beto-o-rourke-launches-2018-senate-cam-paign-in-underdog-bid-to-unseat-ted-cruz/.

"MJ Hegar on Gun Control." *On the Issues,* accessed September 29, 2021. *https://www.ontheissues.org/domestic/MJ_Hegar_Gun_Control.htm.*

"PVF: Defend Freedom. DEFEAT MJ Hegar." *NRA,* accessed September 29, 2021. *https://www.nrapvf.org/campaigns/2020/mj-hegar/.*

Platoff, Emma, and Svitek, Patrick. "Beto O'Rourke Drops out of Presidential Race." *The Texas Tribune,* November 1, 2019. *https://www.texastribune.org/2019/11/01/beto-orourke-drops-out-presidential-race/.*

Samuels, Alex. "Beto O'Rourke's Flock Remains Loyal While His Party Debates Whether to Move On." *The Texas Tribune,* February 11, 2020. *https://www.texastribune.org/2020/02/11/beto-orourke-supporters-texas-democrats/.*

Scherer, Michael. "Beto O'Rourke's Political Career Drew on Donations from THE pro-GOP Business Establishment." *The Texas Tribune,* March 15, 2019. *https://www.texastribune.org/2019/03/15/beto-orourke-drew-donations-pro-gop-polit-ical-establishment/.*

Shepard, Steven, Charlie Mahtesian, David Siders, Christopher Caldelago, Elena Schneider, Ally Mutnik, and Laura Barron-Lopez. "Texas Senate Election Results 2020: Live Map UPDATES: Voting by County." *POLITICO,* accessed

September 29, 2021. *https://www.politico.com/2020-election/results/texas/senate/*.

Svitek, Patrick. "In Getting out the Vote, Cruz Turns To Abbott's Infrastructure While O'Rourke Builds His Own." *The Texas Tribune*, November 1, 2018. *https://www.texastribune.org/2018/11/01/ted-cruz-beto-orourke-get-out-the-vote/*.

Svitek, Patrick. "Ted Cruz Releases First TV Ads of 2018, Including 3 Attacking Beto O'Rourke." *The Texas Tribune*, August 3, 2018. *https://www.texastribune.org/2018/08/03/cruz-orourke-attack-ad-reelection-texas/*.

The Texas Politics Project at University of Texas at Austin. "John Cornyn Job APPROVAL TREND." *The Texas Politics Project*, September 8, 2021. *https://texaspolitics.utexas.edu/set/john-cornyn-job-approval-trend#democratic-identification*.

Yaffe-Bellany, David. "Texas Has 254 Counties. Beto O'Rourke Has Campaigned against Ted Cruz in Each of Them." *The Texas Tribune*, June 9, 2018. *https://www.texastribune.org/2018/06/09/beto-o-rourke-ted-cruz-texas-254-counties/*.

CHAPTER 3

Cawthorn, Madison. "Madison Cawthorn Proposal Instagram." Instagram, December 27, 2019. *https://www.instagram.com/madisoncawthorn/?hl=en*.

Cawthorn, Madison. "This Is Why I Am Objecting to the 2020 Election Results. The Right to Vote in a Free and Fair Election Is the Cornerstone of Our Republic. Attempts to

Undermine This Strike at the Very Heart of a Representative Government 'of, by, and for the People.' I Will Not Be Silent. Pic.twitter.com/mbqx9ltfq6." Twitter. Twitter, December 31, 2020. *https://twitter.com/cawthornfornc/status /1344740360862527494?lang=en.*

Cawthorn, Madison. "Western North Carolina Deserves a Representative That Is Willing to Fight for You. My Opponent Has Continually Dodged and Avoided Debate Invites from Myself and the GOP. What Is She Afraid of? PIC.TWITTER. COM/I3Z4T6OTTP." Twitter. Twitter, June 17, 2020. *https:// twitter.com/cawthornfornc/status/1273264631251906562?l ang=en.*

"Haywood County Republicans Meeting Audio." Box. Accessed October 3, 2021. *https://app.box.com/s/obk9b3423wqksb- frsh2y2viu359aipmc?fbclid=IwAR2TUBeTQQWjWu- FRv8DCSrcDLX1p2k4Wc1ppoORpPoF1KgoHM5fOSSbRMz4.*

Kranish, Michael. "The Making of Madison Cawthorn: How Falsehoods Helped Propel the Career of a New pro-Trump Star of the Far Right." *The Washington Post*, February 27, 2021. *https://www.washingtonpost.com/politics/2021/02/27/ making-madison-cawthorn-how-falsehoods-helped-propel-ca- reer-new-pro-trump-star-far-right/.*

Lightning Reports. "Henderson County Four Seasons Politics: Bennett Dodging Debate, Cawthorn Says" *Hendersonville Lightning*, accessed October 3, 2021. *https://www.henderson- villelightning.com/four-seasons-politics/9293-congress.html.*

"Lynda Bennett." Ballotpedia. Accessed October 3, 2021. *https:// ballotpedia.org/Lynda_Bennett.*

"Madison Cawthorn." Ballotpedia. Accessed October 3, 2021. *https://ballotpedia.org/Madison_Cawthorn.*

Mutnick, Ally. "Inside the Crazy Race to Replace Mark Meadows." *POLITICO,* February 14, 2020. *https://www.politico.com/news/2020/02/14/mark-meadows-race-successor-115106.*

Neumann, Sean. "25-Year-Old Congressman Wasn't Left 'to Die' in Fiery Crash, Says Friend Who Was Driving." *PEOPLE Magazine,* March 3, 2021. *https://people.com/politics/madison-cawthorn-not-left-to-die-in-crash-friend-says/.*

Oprysko, Caitlin. "Trump Congratulates 24-Year-Old Who Upset White House's Chosen Candidate in N.C. Runoff." *POLITICO,* June 25, 2020. *https://www.politico.com/news/2020/06/24/trump-congratulates-madison-cawthorn-337922.*

Perrotti, Kyle. "Trump Weighs in on 11th Congressional Race." *The Mountaineer,* June 5, 2020. *https://www.themountaineer.com/news/trump-weighs-in-on-11th-congressional-race/article_76026916-a675-11ea-a669-b3eca60dacf6.html.*

"Top Conservative Colleges." *Students,* May 20, 2020. *https://students.yaf.org/top-conservative-colleges/.*

CHAPTER 4

"2019 Report Cards All Representatives / Missed Votes." *Gov-Track*, accessed October 3, 2021. *https://www.govtrack.us/congress/members/report-cards/2019/house/missed-votes.*

"Alexandria Ocasio-Cortez—Congress." Accessed October 3, 2021. *https://www.congress.gov/member/alexandria-ocasio-cortez/O000172?r=124.*

"Brenda Jones On The Issues." OnTheIssues.org. Accessed October 3, 2021. *https://www.ontheissues.org/MI/Brenda_Jones.htm.*

"Congressional District 14, NY." *Data USA,* accessed October 3, 2021. *https://datausa.io/profile/geo/congressional-district-14-ny.*

Ferretti , Christine, and Melissa Nann Burke. "Tlaib Wins US House Seat, Becomes among First Muslim-American Women Elected." *The Detroit News,* November 8, 2018. *https://www.detroitnews.com/story/news/politics/elections/2018/11/06/us-house-representatives-thirteenth-district-conyers-tlaib-jones-race-results-winner/1826398002/.*

Goldmacher, Shane, and Jonathan Martin. "Alexandria Ocasio-Cortez Defeats Joseph Crowley in Major Democratic House Upset." *The New York Times,* June 27, 2018. *https://www.nytimes.com/2018/06/26/nyregion/joseph-crowley-ocasio-cortez-democratic-primary.html.*

Harper, Christopher Lee. "Total Raised $34,158,784.96/total Spent $36,437,105.76 @Votesmart on a $174,000 Salary Https://T.co/vg6yapspxblegislaton Passed = 1 @Potus @Joe-

biden o Passed @potus45 #Trump Https://T.co/w558vvdj2p
@Congressdotgov Https://T.co/9igm21iexahttps://T.co/
Ervcrguquyquote Tweet." Twitter. Twitter, August 5, 2021.
https://twitter.com/Charpy73/status/1423363576161570822.

"HR 4508." Congress.Gov. Accessed October 3, 2021. *https://www.
congress.gov/bill/116th-congress/house-bill/4508?s=6&r=1.*

"Ilhan Omar ." Congress.Gov. Accessed October 3, 2021. *https://
www.congress.gov/member/ilhan-omar/O000173?searchRe-
sultViewType=expanded&pageSize=100&q=%7B%22bill-sta-
tus%22%3A%22law%22%7D.*

Jaffe, Greg, and Souad Mekhennet. "Ilhan Omar's American
Story: It's Complicated." *The Washington Post,* July 6, 2019.
*https://www.washingtonpost.com/politics/2019/07/06/ilhan-
omar-is-unlike-anyone-who-has-served-congress-this-is-her-
complicated-american-story/.*

Mays, Jeffery C. "Ocasio-Cortez Wins 2nd Term in Costly Loss
for Republicans." *The New York Times,* November 4, 2020.
*https://www.nytimes.com/2020/11/03/nyregion/ny-house-aoc.
html.*

"Michigan's 13th Congressional District Election (August 7, 2018
Republican Primary)." Ballotpedia. Accessed October 3,
2021. *https://ballotpedia.org/Michigan%27s_13th_Congressio-
nal_District_election_(August_7,_2018_Republican_primary).*

Moore, Elena. "Rep. Ilhan Omar Wins Congressional
Primary." *NPR,* August 12, 2020. *https://www.npr.*

org/2020/08/11/901429697/rep-ilhan-omar-wins-congressional-primary.

Murray, Mark. "Huge Turnout in Ayanna Pressley's Victory over Michael Capuano." *NBC News,* September 5, 2018. *https://www.nbcnews.com/card/turnout-huge-ayanna-pressley-s-victory-over-michael-capuano-n906556?cid=sm_npd_nn_tw_mtp.*

Paz, Isabella Grullón. "Rashida Tlaib Won a Primary This Week. She Also Lost a Primary This Week." *The New York Times,* August 9, 2018. *https://www.nytimes.com/2018/08/09/us/politics/rashida-tlaib-brenda-jones.html.*

"Rashida Tlaib—Congress." Accessed October 3, 2021. *https://www.congress.gov/member/rashida-tlaib/T000481?searchResultViewType=expanded&pageSize=100&page=2.*

"Rep. Ilhan Omar Releases Progress Report of Her Tenure in Congress." Representative Ilhan Omar, August 22, 2019. *https://omar.house.gov/media/press-releases/rep-ilhan-omar-releases-progress-report-her-tenure-congress.*

"Rooted in Community." Rashida For Congress, January 28, 2021. *https://rashidaforcongress.com/rooted-in-community/.*

Salsberg, Bob. "Democrats Capuano, Pressley Spar over Advocacy, Leadership in Debate." *The Boston Globe,* August 7, 2018. *https://www.boston.com/news/local-news/2018/08/07/democrats-capuano-pressley-spar-over-advocacy-leadership-in-debate.*

Schneider, Gabe. "What Antone Melton-Meaux's Primary Challenge to Ilhan Omar Is All About." *MinnPost*, July 11, 2020. *https://www.minnpost.com/national/2020/07/what-antone-melton-meauxs-primary-challenge-to-ilhan-omar-is-all-about/.*

"Send Her Back." Ilhan Omar for Congress. Accessed October 3, 2021. *https://ilhanomar.com/thefacts/.*

CHAPTER 5

"About." Young Republican National Federation. August 8, 2021. *https://yrnf.com/about/.*

"Colorado's 3rd Congressional District Election, 2020 (June 30 Republican Primary)." Ballotpedia. Accessed October 3, 2021. *https://ballotpedia.org/Colorado%27s_3rd_Congressional_District_election,_2020_(June_30_Republican_primary).*

"Committee Assignments." Senator Josh Hawley. Accessed October 3, 2021. *https://www.hawley.senate.gov/committee-assignments.*

Dixon, Matt. "Matt Gaetz Announces Run for Congress, Will Spend Personal Money." *Politico PRO,* March 21, 2016. *https://www.politico.com/states/florida/story/2016/03/matt-gaetz-announces-run-for-congress-will-spend-personal-money-032589.*

Editorial Board. "Editorial: Hawley Should Resign. Silent Enablers Must Now Publicly Condemn Trumpism." *STLtoday.com,* January 22, 2021. *https://www.stltoday.com/opinion/editorial/editorial-hawley-should-resign-silent-en-*

*ablers-must-now-publicly-condemn-trumpism/article_*
beae190c-9c42-5c18-bb54-e3e3877192d7.html.

"Electeds." Young Republican National Federation, June 3, 2021.
https://yrnf.com/electeds/.

Full Interview: Shooters Grill Owner Lauren ...—Youtube." Youtube. Next9News, December 9, 2019. *https://www.youtube.*
com/watch?v=ql2iKm9tZCk.

Hancock, Jason, Anita Kumar, and Bryan Lowry. "Trump Urges
Missouri Supporters to Back...—Kansascity.com." The Kansas City Star, September 28, 2018. *https://www.kansascity.*
com/news/politics-government/article218799850.html.

Itkowitz, Colby, Felicia Sonmez, John Wagner, Amy B. Wang,
and Marisa Iati. "Pelosi, Schumer Call for Trump's Removal;
Trump Acknowledges New Administration." *The Washing-*
ton Post, January 8, 2021. *https://www.washingtonpost.com/*
politics/2021/01/07/congress-election-biden-capitol-live-up-
dates/#link-X3H54PQ72RE7ZBHOVHF42UBQ2M.

"Josh Hawley." Ballotpedia. Accessed October 3, 2021. *https://*
ballotpedia.org/Josh_Hawley.

"Josh Hawley Congress.Gov Records." Congress.Gov. Accessed
October 3, 2021. *https://www.congress.gov/member/josh-haw-*
ley/H001089?searchResultViewType=expanded&page-
Size=100&q=%7B%22bill-status%22%3A%22law%22%7D.

Kansas City Star Editorial Board. "Mo Sen Josh Hawley Should
Resign after Riot at the Capitol." *Kansas City Star*, January

8, 2021. *https://www.kansascity.com/opinion/editorials/article248349315.html.*

Keller, Rudi. "Major Josh Hawley Donor Calls for Him to Be Censured by the US Senate." *Missouri Independent,* January 8, 2021. *https://missouriindependent.com/2021/01/07/major-josh-hawley-donor-calls-for-him-to-be-censured-by-the-u-s-senate/.*

Kinzinger, Adam. "Matt Gaetz Needs to Resign." Twitter. Twitter, April 9, 2021. *https://twitter.com/AdamKinzinger/status/1380334741682073603?ref_src=twsrc%5Etfw%7Ctwcamp%5Etweetembed%7Ctwterm%5E138033 4741682073603%7Ctwgr%5E%7Ctwcon%5Es1_&ref_url=https%3A%2F%2Fwww.npr.org%2F2021%2F04%2F0 9%2F985851957%2Fhouse-ethics-committee-investigating-florida-gop-rep-matt-gaetz.*

Lowry, Bryan. "Poll Shows Hawley Has Negative Approval Rating in Missouri—the Kansas City Star." The Kansas City Star, January 2021. *https://www.kansascity.com/news/politics-government/article248701795.html.*

"Matt Gaetz." Congress.Gov. Accessed October 3, 2021. *https://www.congress.gov/member/matt-gaetz/G000578?searchResultViewType=expanded&pageSize=100&q=%7B%22bill-status%22%3A%22law%22%7D.*

"Matt Gaetz Abortion." Matt Gaetz on Abortion. Accessed October 3, 2021. *https://www.ontheissues.org/FL/Matt_Gaetz_Abortion.htm.*

"Matt Gaetz Immigration." Matt Gaetz on Immigration. Accessed October 3, 2021. *https://www.ontheissues.org/FL/Matt_Gaetz_Immigration.htm*.

"Matt Gaetz War and Peace." Matt Gaetz on War & Peace. Accessed October 3, 2021. *https://www.ontheissues.org/FL/Matt_Gaetz_War_+_Peace.htm*

"Meet Matt." Gaetz for Congress. Accessed October 3, 2021. *https://www.mattgaetz.com/meet-matt*.

Messenger, Tony, and C-Span. "Messenger: Danforth Calls His Support of Hawley the 'Worst Mistake' of His Life." *STLtoday.com*, April 22, 2021. *https://www.stltoday.com/news/local/columns/tony-messenger/messenger-danforth-calls-his-support-of-hawley-the-worst-mistake-of-his-life/article_0f8288fc-4b22-5fe7-8cb9-d29161a7cf81.html*.

Miles, James Robert, Ron Ogden, Tjb, Ocean Joe, Demetries, Andrew DeGeorge, and James Connor. "Poll Finds Majority of GOP Voters in Matt Gaetz's District Still Stand with Him." *Florida Politics,* April 11, 2021. *https://floridapolitics.com/archives/419120-poll-finds-majority-of-republicans-in-matt-gaetzs-home-district-stand-with-him/*.

Mizzou Law Student Bar Association. "The Student Bar Association of Mizzou Law Calls on Senator Hawley to Resign for the Sake of Our State, for the Benefit of Our Country, but Most Importantly, for the Protection of the Rule of Law. Pic.twitter.com/qkdz9oamag." Twitter. Twitter, January 7, 2021. *https://twitter.com/MULawSBA/status/1347022216676990981?s=20*.

Sprunt, Barbara, and Deirdre Walsh. "House Ethics Committee Investigating GOP Rep. Matt Gaetz of Florida." *NPR*, April 10, 2021. *https://www.npr.org/2021/04/09/985851957/house-ethics-committee-investigating-florida-gop-rep-matt-gaetz.*

Staff Reports. "'Absolute Warrior' Matt Gaetz Wins Primary in Panhandle's CD 1." *Florida Politics,* August 29, 2018. *https://floridapolitics.com/archives/272324-matt-gaetz-wins-cd-1/.*

CHAPTER 6

Budryk, Zack. "Abrams Says Concession Comparisons to Trump Are 'Apples to Bowling Balls'." *The Hill*, January 3, 2021. *https://thehill.com/homenews/sunday-talk-shows/532413-abrams-says-comparing-her-gubernatorial-challenge-to-trumps.*

Cramer, Philissa, et al. "Jon Ossoff: Everything You Need to Know about the New Jewish Democratic Senator." *The Times of Israel,* January 8, 2021. *https://www.timesofisrael.com/jon-ossoff-everything-you-need-to-know-about-the-new-jewish-democratic-senator/.*

"David Perdue." *Encyclopædia Britannica,* Accessed October 3, 2021. *https://www.britannica.com/biography/David-Perdue.*

Durkin, Erin. "GOP Candidate Improperly Purged 340,000 from Georgia Voter Rolls, Investigation Claims." *Guardian News and Media,* October 19, 2018. *https://www.theguardian.com/us-news/2018/oct/19/georgia-governor-race-voter-suppression-brian-kemp.*

Fedor, Lauren. "Stacey Abrams: The Political Strategist Who Won Georgia." *Financial Times,* January 8, 2021. *https://www. ft.com/content/8af50180-bbab-4595-a32b-fe9af205f1ce.*

Fowler, Stephen. "Kemp Signs 98-Page Omnibus Elections Bill." *Georgia Public Broadcasting* Accessed October 3, 2021. *https:// www.gpb.org/news/2021/03/25/kemp-signs-98-page-omnibus-elections-bill.*

"Georgia Election: Who Is Reverend Raphael Warnock?" *BBC News,* January 6, 2021. *https://www.bbc.com/news/election-us-2020-55559966.*

Hutton, Alice. "Biden Touts Stacey Abrams as a Future Presidential Candidate in a Speech in Georgia." *The Independent,* April 30, 2021. *https://www.independent.co.uk/news/world/americas/us-politics/biden-abrams-president-b1840418.html.*

Johnson, Katanga, and Heather Timmons. "How Stacey Abrams Paved the Way for a Democratic Victory in 'New Georgia'." *Reuters,* November 10, 2020. *https://www.reuters.com/article/us-usa-election-georgia/how-stacey-abrams-paved-the-way-for-a-democratic-victory-in-new-georgia-idUSKBN27P17F.*

Kara Brandeisky, Hanqing Chen. "Everything That's Happened since Supreme Court Ruled on Voting Rights Act." ProPublica. Accessed October 3, 2021. *https://www.propublica.org/article/voting-rights-by-state-map.*

Khalid, Asma. "Stacey vs. Stacey: The Democratic Fight for Governor in Georgia." *NPR,* May 21, 2018. *https://www.npr.*

org/2018/05/21/612323600/stacey-vs-stacey-the-democrat-ic-fight-for-governor-in-georgia.

Lea, Brittany De. "Who Is Kelly Loeffler? 4 Things to Know about the Georgia Senator." *Fox News*, January 4, 2021. *https://www.foxnews.com/politics/kelly-loeffler-4-things-to-know-georgia-senator.*

Liptak, Adam. "Supreme Court Invalidates Key Part of Voting Rights Act." *The New York Times*, June 25, 2013. *https://www.nytimes.com/2013/06/26/us/supreme-court-ruling.html.*

Natalie Dreier, Cox Media Group National Content Desk. "Who Is Senator-Elect Jon Ossoff? 5 Things to Know." *KIRO 7 News Seattle,* January 6, 2021. *https://www.kiro7.com/news/trending/who-is-jon-ossoff-5-things-know/V4HH5NO2JVCL-DEA5AIK4AMYIJI/.*

"Rep. Stacey Abrams D-89 Biography—Georgia." Georgia House. Accessed October 3, 2021. *https://www.house.ga.gov/Documents/Biographies/abramsStacey.pdf.*

Seitz-Wald, Alex. "Stacey Abrams Wins Georgia 'Battle of the Staceys' in Bid to Become First Black Female Governor in US." *NBC News*, May 23, 2018. *https://www.nbcnews.com/politics/elections/stacey-abrams-wins-georgia-battle-staceys-bid-become-first-black-n876616.*

Shelby v Holder (*https://www.supremecourt.gov/opinions/12pdf/12-96_6k47.pdf* June 25, 2013). "Voter Fraud Map: Election Fraud Database." The Heritage Foundation. Accessed October 3, 2021. *https://www.heritage.org/voterfraud/*

search?state=GA&combine=&year=&case_type=All&fraud_type=All&page=0.

CHAPTER 7

"2020 Census Frequently Asked Questions." The Data Center. Accessed October 4, 2021. *https://www.data-centerresearch.org/2020-census-resources/2020-census-frequently-asked-questions/.*

"A Boycott of the 2020 Census." Americanbar.org. American Bar Association. Accessed October 4, 2021. *https://www.americanbar.org/news/abanews/aba-news-archives/2019/07/a-boycott-of-the-2020-census/.*

Colby, Clifford. "Your US Census Response Is Required. Here Are Three Ways to Fill out Your Form." *CNET,* April 3, 2020. *https://www.cnet.com/how-to/your-us-census-response-is-required-here-are-three-ways-to-fill-out-your-form/.*

"Counting for Dollars 2020—The George Washington University." Accessed October 4, 2021. *https://gwipp.gwu.edu/sites/g/files/zaxdzs2181/f/downloads/Counting%20for%20Dollars%20 2020%20-%20Comprehensive%20Accounting_Report%20 7B%20Feb%202020%20rev.pdf.*

"Digest of Education Statistics, 2010." National Center for Education Statistics. Accessed October 4, 2021. *https://nces.ed.gov/programs/digest/d10/tables/dt10_103.asp.*

Frey, William H. "What the 2020 Census Will Reveal about America: Stagnating Growth, an Aging Population, and

Youthful Diversity." *Brookings,* July 12, 2021. *https://www.brookings.edu/research/what-the-2020-census-will-reveal-about-america-stagnating-growth-an-aging-population-and-youthful-diversity/.*

Griffith, Michelle. "Why Are Rural North Dakotans Not Responding to the 2020 Census?" *The Dickinson Press,* August 24, 2020. *https://www.thedickinsonpress.com/news/government-and-politics/6629431-Why-are-rural-North-Dakotans-not-responding-to-the-2020-census.*

Hoffower, Hillary. "Women Are Taking a 'Rain Check' on Babies, and It Could Change the Shape of the Economy." *Business Insider,* April 18, 2021. *https://www.businessinsider.com/pandemic-baby-bust-could-slow-down-economy-millennials-delaying-kids-2021-4.*

Moulton, Sean, and Steven Long. "The Importance of the 2020 Census, Explained in Dollars and Cents." Project On Government Oversight. Accessed October 4, 2021. *https://www.pogo.org/analysis/2020/03/the-importance-of-the-2020-census-explained-in-dollars-and-cents/.*

"National Teacher and Principal Survey (NTPS)." National Center for Education Statistics (NCES). National Center for Education Statistics (NCES), 2018. *https://nces.ed.gov/surveys/ntps/tables/ntps1718_fltable06_t1s.asp.*

"Party Control of Texas State Government." Ballotpedia. Accessed October 4, 2021. *https://ballotpedia.org/Party_control_of_Texas_state_government.*

"SEAA Immigrants Census Confidentiality and the …—SEARAC." The Southeast Asia Resource Action Center. Accessed October 4, 2021. *https://www.searac.org/wp-content/uploads/2019/08/SEAA-Immigrants-Census-Confidentiality-and-the-Citizenship-Question_FINAL-FINAL.pdf.*

Tara Bahrampour, Harry Stevens. "2020 Census Shows US Population Grew at Slowest Pace Since the 1930s." *The Washington Post,* April 27, 2021. *https://www.washingtonpost.com/dc-md-va/interactive/2021/2020-census-us-population-results/.*

Tausanovitch, Jasmine Hardy and Alex. "How to Fix Gerrymandering." Center for American Progress, July 26, 2019. *https://www.americanprogress.org/issues/democracy/news/2019/07/26/472791/how-to-fix-gerrymandering/.*

"US Census Bureau Quickfacts: Rhode Island." Accessed October 4, 2021. *https://www.census.gov/quickfacts/RI.*

"Why Does the Census Matter?" Council on Foreign Relations. Accessed October 4, 2021. *https://www.cfr.org/backgrounder/why-does-census-matter.*

CHAPTER 8

Ashare, Rebecca L., Catherine J. Norris, E. Paul Wileyto, John T. Cacioppo, and Andrew A. Strasser. "Individual Differences in Positivity Offset and Negativity Bias: Gender-Specific Associations with Two Serotonin Receptor Genes." US National Library of Medicine, September 1, 2013. *https://www.ncbi.nlm.nih.gov/pmc/articles/PMC3747009/.*

Baxter, Mark G. and Paula L. Croxson. "Facing the Role of the Amygdala in Emotional Information Processing." National Academy of Sciences, December 26, 2012. *https://www.pnas.org/content/109/52/21180.*

"Beto O'Rourke on Tax Reform." On The Issues. Accessed October 5, 2021. *https://www.ontheissues.org/2020/Beto_O%60Rourke_Tax_Reform.htm.*

Biden, Joe. "This Is Our Moment to Choose: Hope over Fear. Unity over Division. Science over Fiction. Truth over Lies. Vote: Https://T.co/e0xt07d7qb." Twitter. Twitter, November 3, 2020. *https://twitter.com/JoeBiden/status/1323722695297695745.*

Biden, Joe. "This Is Our Moment to Prove That: Love Is More Powerful than Hate. Hope Is More Powerful than Fear. Light Is More Powerful than Dark. Vote before Polls Close: Https://T.co/e0xt07d7qb." Twitter. Twitter, November 3, 2020. *https://twitter.com/JoeBiden/status/1323753975221522433.*

Brassil, Gillian R., and Jeré Longman. "Who Should Compete in Women's Sports? There Are 'Two Almost Irreconcilable Positions'." *The New York Times,* August 18, 2020. *https://www.nytimes.com/2020/08/18/sports/transgender-athletes-womens-sports-idaho.html.*

Bycoffe. "Tracking Congress in the Age of Trump." *FiveThirtyEight,* January 13, 2021. *https://projects.fivethirtyeight.com/congress-trump-score/liz-cheney/.*

Castronuovo, Celine. "50 Percent of Republican Voters Say Cheney Should Lose Leadership Position: Poll." *The Hill,* May 12, 2021. *https://thehill.com/homenews/house/553033-50-percent-of-republican-voters-say-cheney-should-lose-leadership-position.*

Cawthorn, Madison. "True Patriots Must Call Out These Fake Republicans. We Are in a Fight against Communism That Is Threatening to Take over Our Nation. We Must Unify. Liz Cheney Is Fracturing This Movement & Allowing the Roots of Socialism to Take Hold. Liz Cheney Must Go. Pic.twitter.com/gf2do5kata." Twitter. Twitter, May 5, 2021. *https://twitter.com/CawthornforNC/status/1390044558319308800.*

Crary, David. "Lawmakers Can't Cite Local Examples of Trans Girls in Sports." *Associated Press,* March 3, 2021. *https://apnews.com/article/lawmakers-unable-to-cite-local-trans-girls-sports-914a982545e943ecc1e265e8c41042e7.*

D., Dodd Michael, Amanda Balzer, Carly M. Jacobs, et al. "The Political Left Rolls with the Good and the Political Right Confronts the Bad: Connecting Physiology and Cognition to Preferences." Philosophical Transactions of the Royal Society B: Biological Sciences, March 5, 2012. *http://rstb.royalsocietypublishing.org/content/367/1589/640.full#aff-1.*

"'Drug Dealers, Criminals, Rapists': What Trump Thinks of Mexicans." *BBC News,* August 31, 2016. *https://www.bbc.com/news/av/world-us-canada-37230916.*

Fagan, Abigail. "Fear and Anxiety Drive Conservatives' Political Attitudes." *Psychology Today,* December 31, 2016. *https://www.*

psychologytoday.com/us/blog/mind-in-the-machine/201612/ fear-and-anxiety-drive-conservatives-political-attitudes.

Fox Business Network. "Willie Robertson: There's No Crying in Politics." YouTube. YouTube, November 14, 2016. *https:// www.youtube.com/watch?v=oEMnbw6ries.*

Frye, Devon. "Psychology of the Non-Voter Personality Type." *Psychology Today,* October 27, 2020. *https://www.psycholo- gytoday.com/us/blog/personality-quotient/202010/psycholo- gy-the-non-voter-personality-type.*

Herbert, Wray. "Red Mind, Blue Mind: Are There Any Real Inde- pendents?" Association for Psychological Science—APS, May 25, 2012. *https://www.psychologicalscience.org/news/were-on- ly-human/red-mind-blue-mind-are-there-any-real-indepen- dents.html.*

"Idaho Proposition 2, Medicaid Expansion Initiative (2018)." Bal- lotpedia. Accessed October 5, 2021. *https://ballotpedia.org/ Idaho_Proposition_2,_Medicaid_Expansion_Initiative_(2018).*

"Liz Cheney." Ballotpedia. Accessed October 5, 2021. *https://bal- lotpedia.org/Liz_Cheney.*

"Nebraska Initiative 427, Medicaid Expansion Initiative (2018)." Ballotpedia. Accessed October 5, 2021. *https://ballotpedia. org/Nebraska_Initiative_427,_Medicaid_Expansion_Initia- tive_(2018).*

Newport, Frank. "Public Opinion of the War in Afghanistan." Gallup.com. Gallup, April 3, 2021. *https://news.gallup.com/poll/9994/public-opinion-war-afghanistan.aspx.*

Oxley DR; Smith KB; Alford JR; Hibbing MV; Miller JL; Scalora M; Hatemi PK; Hibbing JR. "Political Attitudes Vary with Physiological Traits." Science (New York, N.Y.). US National Library of Medicine. Accessed October 5, 2021. *https://pubmed.ncbi.nlm.nih.gov/18801995/.*

Oyeniyi, Doyin. "Bathroom Bills Are Creating More Issues than They Claim to Solve." *Texas Monthly,* May 19, 2016. *https://www.texasmonthly.com/the-daily-post/bathroom-bills-creating-issues-claim-solve/.*

"Projectimplicit." About the IAT. Accessed October 5, 2021. *https://implicit.harvard.edu/implicit/iatdetails.html.*

"Remarks Accepting the Presidential Nomination at the Republican National Convention in Houston." *The American Presidency Project,* August 20, 1992. *https://www.presidency.ucsb.edu/documents/remarks-accepting-the-presidential-nomination-the-republican-national-convention-houston.*

"Remarks by the President on Comprehensive Immigration Reform." National Archives and Records Administration. Accessed October 5, 2021. *https://obamawhitehouse.archives.gov/the-press-office/remarks-president-comprehensive-immigration-reform.*

Soichet, Catherine. "They Crossed the US Border with Explosives — from Canada ...," January 8, 2019. *https://www.cnn.com/2019/01/08/us/us-canada-border-terror/index.html*.

Spring, Marianna. "'Stop the Steal': The Deep Roots of Trump's 'Voter Fraud' Strategy." *BBC News,* November 23, 2020. *https://www.bbc.com/news/blogs-trending-55009950*.

"Transcript of George W. Bush's Acceptance Speech ." *ABC News,* January 6, 2006. *https://abcnews.go.com/Politics/story?id=123214&page=1*.

"Transcript of Speech by Clinton Accepting Democratic Nomination." *The New York Times,* July 17, 1992. *https://www.nytimes.com/1992/07/17/news/their-own-words-transcript-speech-clinton-accepting-democratic-nomination.html*.

"Transcript: Barack Obama's Acceptance Speech." *NPR,* August 29, 2008. *https://www.npr.org/templates/story/story.php?storyId=94087570*.

"Transcript: 'This Is Your Victory,' Says Obama." *Cable News Network,* November 4, 2008. *https://edition.cnn.com/2008/POLITICS/11/04/obama.transcript/*.

"Utah Proposition 3, Medicaid Expansion Initiative (2018)." Ballotpedia. Accessed October 5, 2021. *https://ballotpedia.org/Utah_Proposition_3,_Medicaid_Expansion_Initiative_(2018)*.

Vaish, Amrisha, Tobias Grossmann, and Amanda Woodward. "Not All Emotions Are Created Equal: The Negativity Bias in Social-Emotional Development." US National Library of Medicine, May 2008. *https://www.ncbi.nlm.nih.gov/pmc/articles/PMC3652533/.*

Valentino, Nicholas. "Election Night's Alright for Fighting the Role of Emotions …" Accessed October 5, 2021. *https://www.researchgate.net/profile/Nicholas-Valentino/publication/231894452_Election_Night%27s_Alright_for_Fighting_The_Role_of_Emotions_in_Political_Participation/links/54c78f5b0cf22d626a369b1d/Election-Nights-Alright-for-Fighting-The-Role-of-Emotions-in-Political-Participation.pdf.*

"Why Liberals Are More Open to Experience than Conservatives." *Psychology Today,* December 12, 2020. *https://www.psychologytoday.com/us/blog/unique-everybody-else/202012/why-liberals-are-more-open-experience-conservatives.*

Zarroli, Jim. "US Economy Grew 2.9 Percent in 2018, Just below Trump's Target." *NPR,* February 28, 2019. *https://www.npr.org/2019/02/28/698884578/u-s-economy-grew-2-9-percent-in-2018-just-below-trumps-target.*

CHAPTER 9

Apple, Inc. "ITunesCharts.net: 'Blueneck' by Chris Housman (American …" iTunes Charts. Accessed October 5, 2021. *http://www.itunescharts.net/us/artists/music/chris-housman/songs/blueneck/.*

Center for Disease Control and Prevention. "Products—Data Briefs—Number 388- October 2020." October 20, 2020. *https://www.cdc.gov/nchs/products/databriefs/db388.htm.*

Lyons, Linda. "Teens Stay True to Parents' Political Perspectives." *Gallup,* April 3, 2021. *https://news.gallup.com/poll/14515/teens-stay-true-parents-political-perspectives.aspx.*

CHAPTER 10

"About Us." League of Women Voters. Accessed October 5, 2021. *https://www.lwv.org/about-us.*

"Election Impact Report 2020." League of Women Voters. Accessed October 5, 2021. *https://www.lwv.org/sites/default/files/2021-05/LWV_ElectionImpactReport_2020.pdf.*

Flynn, Meagan. "Warren Joked about Her Dog Voting Democrat. GOP Officials Insist Electoral Pet Fraud Is No Laughing Matter." *The Washington Post,* July 17, 2020. *https://www.washingtonpost.com/nation/2020/07/17/dogs-voting-biden-trump/.*

"Jeanette Senecal: League of Women Voters." League of Women Voters. Accessed October 5, 2021. *https://www.lwv.org/about-us/staff-leadership/jeanette-senecal.*

Lyons, Dylan. "How Many People Speak Spanish, and Where Is It Spoken?" *Babbel Magazine,* March 9, 2020. *https://www.babbel.com/en/magazine/how-many-people-speak-spanish-and-where-is-it-spoken.*

McGee, Lilly. "Your Guide to Mis- and Disinformation." League of Women Voters, July 12, 2021. *https://www.lwv.org/blog/your-guide-mis-and-disinformation.*

Pew Research Center. "The 2020 Voting Experience: Corona-
    virus, Mail Concerns Factored into Deciding How to Vote."
    Pew Research Center—US Politics & Policy. December
    5, 2020. *https://www.pewresearch.org/politics/2020/11/20/
    the-voting-experience-in-2020/.*

Solomón, Virginia Kase. "Remaining Nonpartisan in Hyper-Par-
    tisan Times." League of Women Voters, February 10, 2021.
    *https://www.lwv.org/blog/remaining-nonpartisan-hyper-par-
    tisan-times.*

CHAPTER 11

"Alexandria Ocasio-Cortez Says Abortion Bans Are a 'Brutal
    Form of Oppression' and Are About 'Owning Women.'"
    10TV (CBS News), May 16, 2019. *https://www.10tv.com/article/
    news/nation-world/alexandria-ocasio-cortez-says-abortion-
    bans-are-brutal-form-oppression-and-are-about-owning/530-
    59196742-fb5b-42d7-85dc-5ea3f20289bd.*

Assistant Secretary for Public Affairs. "New HHS Data Show
    More Americans than Ever Have Health Coverage through
    the Affordable Care Act." HHS.gov, June 8, 2021. *https://www.
    hhs.gov/about/news/2021/06/05/new-hhs-data-show-more-
    americans-than-ever-have-health-coverage-through-afford-
    able-care-act.html.*

Christensen, Jen. "The Most Common Pre-Existing Medical
    Conditions." CNN. Cable News Network, September 21,
    2017. *https://www.cnn.com/2017/09/20/health/most-com-
    mon-pre-existing-conditions/index.html.*

Digital Communications Division. "Can I Get Coverage If I Have a Pre-Existing Condition?" HHS.gov, August 4, 2017. *https://www.hhs.gov/answers/affordable-care-act/can-i-get-coverage-if-i-have-a-pre-existing-condition/index.html.*

Hawkes, Logan. "You're Going to Take Away My What? Not in Texas." Texas Less Traveled. Texas Less Traveled. Accessed October 5, 2021. *http://texaslesstraveled.com/gunrights.htm.*

Neifach, Michael, and Kimberly Bennett. "Manufacturing Industry's Labor Shortage and Immigrant Workers." *The National Law Review,* March 4, 2021. *https://www.natlaw-review.com/article/manufacturing-industry-s-labor-short-age-and-immigrant-workers.*

Parker, Kim, Juliana Menasce Horowitz, Ruth Igielnik, J. Baxter Oliphant, and Anna Brown. "Guns in America: Attitudes and Experiences of Americans." Pew Research Center, May 30, 2020. *https://www.pewresearch.org/social-trends/2017/06/22/americas-complex-relationship-with-guns/.*

Staff, Indy. "Labor Shortage Leaves $13 Million in Crops to Rot in Fields." *The Santa Barbara Independent,* June 22, 2017. *https://www.independent.com/2017/06/22/labor-shortage-leaves-13-million-crops-rot-fields/.*

CHAPTER 12

Butler, Jada. "George W Bush Reveals He Voted for Condoleezza Rice in 2020 US Election." *The Guardian,* April 23, 2021. *https://www.theguardian.com/us-news/2021/apr/23/george-w-bush-2020-presidential-election-vote-condoleezza-rice.*

Department of Homeland Security. "US Naturalizations: 2019—
Annual Flow Report August 2020." Accessed October 5,
2021. *https://www.dhs.gov/sites/default/files/publications/
immigration-statistics/yearbook/2019/naturalizations_2019.
pdf?fbclid=IwAR099FT1oR2gt_5uIVNWuZZ8ejp2wfsof3rL-
LOaV8YLayeNlQnbYerR3gMY.*

Frey, William H. "Turnout in 2020 Election Spiked among Both
Democratic and Republican Voting Groups, New Census
Data Shows." *Brookings,* May 11, 2021. *https://www.brookings.
edu/research/turnout-in-2020-spiked-among-both-democratic-
and-republican-voting-groups-new-census-data-shows/.*

Gurung, Anuj. "'I Have a Home That I Was Born into, and I
Have a Home That I Have Built Here in the US" *New Americans Campaign,* accessed October 5, 2021. *https://www.
newamericanscampaign.org/anuj-garung-i-have-a-home-that-
i-was-born-into-and-i-have-a-home-that-i-have-built-here-in-
the-u-s/.*

Jillian Blake, J.D. "At What Point in the Naturalization (Citizenship) Process Can I Vote in a US Election?" *Nolo,* August
6, 2020. *https://www.nolo.com/legal-encyclopedia/at-what-
point-in-the-naturalization-citizenship-process-can-i-vote-in-
a-u-s-election.html.*

Montanaro, Domenico. "Poll: Despite Record Turnout, 80 Million Americans Didn't Vote. Here's Why." *NPR,* December 15,
2020. *https://www.npr.org/2020/12/15/945031391/poll-despite-
record-turnout-80-million-americans-didnt-vote-heres-why.*

National Center for Education Statistics. "Public High School Graduation Rates." Accessed October 5, 2021. *https://nces. ed.gov/programs/coe/indicator/coi.*

"New Citizens." Los Angeles County Registrar-Recorder/ County Clerk. Accessed October 5, 2021. *https://www.lavote. net/home/voting-elections/voter-registration/voter-registra- tion-programs/new-citizens.*

CHAPTER 13

"2011, The Year of the Recall." *Los Angeles Times,* December 27, 2011. *https://www.latimes.com/opinion/la-xpm-2011-dec-27- la-oe-spivak-recall-20111227-story.html.*

Andrews, Wilson, and Thomas Kaplan. "Where the Candi- dates Stand on 2016's Biggest Issues." *The New York Times,* December 15, 2015. *https://www.nytimes.com/interactive/2016/ us/elections/candidates-on-the-issues.html.*

Anonymous Author. "Meet the 12 GOP Senators Who Voted to Terminate Trump's National Emergency." *Roll Call,* December 13, 2019. *https://www.rollcall.com/2019/03/14/ meet-the-12-gop-senators-who-voted-to-terminate-trumps- national-emergency/.*

Bacon, Perry. "The Republican Party Has Changed Dramatically since George H.W. Bush Ran It."*FiveThirtyEight,* December 1, 2018. *https://fivethirtyeight.com/features/the-republican-par- ty-has-changed-dramatically-since-george-h-w-bush-ran-it/.*

Barro, Josh. "Four States Vote to Raise Minimum Wage." *The New York Times,* November 3, 2014. *https://www.nytimes. com/2014/11/05/upshot/election-results-2014-minimum-wage. html.*

"California Governor Recall Election Results 2021: Live Map Updates: Voting by County." *POLITICO,* Accessed October 5, 2021. *https://www.politico.com/election-results/2021/ california/gubernatorial-recall/.*

Glass, Andrew. "Schwarzenegger Elected California's Governor, Oct. 7, 2003." *POLITICO,* October 7, 2017. *https://www. politico.com/story/2017/10/07/schwarzenegger-elected-californias-governor-oct-7-2003-243512.*

"Gray Davis Recall, Governor of California (2003)." Ballotpedia. Accessed October 5, 2021. *https://ballotpedia.org/Gray_Davis_ recall_(2003).*

"GSS General Social Survey." NORC. Accessed October 5, 2021. *http://gss.norc.org/.*

"History of Marijuana on the Ballot." Ballotpedia. Accessed October 5, 2021. *https://ballotpedia.org/History_of_marijuana_on_the_ballot.*

Jacobs, Ben. "America's Most Important (and Wackiest) Referendums This November." *The Daily Beast,* April 14, 2017. *https:// www.thedailybeast.com/americas-most-important-and-wackiest-referendums-this-november.*

King, Ledyard. "Bernie Sanders Drops out of Presidential Race, Saying He Concluded His Path to Victory Was 'Virtually Impossible'." *USA Today,* April 8, 2020. *https://www.usatoday.com/story/news/politics/elections/2020/04/08/bernie-sanders-drops-out-2020-presidential-race-joe-biden-surges/4919641002/.*

Leatherby, Lauren, and Sarah Almukhtar. "Democratic Delegate Count and Primary Election Results 2020." *The New York Times,* February 3, 2020. *https://www.nytimes.com/interactive/2020/us/elections/delegate-count-primary-results.html.*

"Maine Voters Reject Ban on Bear Hunting Practices for Second Time." *Bangor Daily News,* November 2, 2015. *https://bangordailynews.com/2014/11/04/news/maine-voters-reject-ban-on-bear-hunting-practices-for-second-time/.*

"Primary Election Systems." NCSL. NCSL. Accessed October 5, 2021. *https://www.ncsl.org/documents/Elections/Primary_Types_Table_2017.pdf.*

Seelye, Katharine Q. "For Gray Davis, Great Fall from the Highest Height." *The New York Times,* October 8, 2003. *https://www.nytimes.com/2003/10/08/us/california-recall-governor-for-gray-davis-great-fall-highest-height.html.*

Strauss, Daniel, Rachana Pradhan, and KRISTEN EAST and DANIEL STRAUSS. "GOP: Sanders Pushed Clinton toward Radical Left." *POLITICO,* July 12, 2016. *https://www.politico.com/story/2016/07/bernie-sanders-democratic-platform-225375.*

The Late Show with Stephen Colbert. "Lucifer In The Flesh"—
    Former Speaker Boehner Unloads On Sen. Ted Cruz. April
    13, 2021. Video, 11:06. *https://www.youtube.com/watch?v=oI-
    r1aJqILcE*.

"The Sanders Manifesto." *POLITICO,* Accessed October 5, 2021.
    *https://www.politico.com/f/?id=00000155-dc41-dfod-a357-
    dc4b4dcf0001*.

"UCLA Presents Voteview.com Beta." Voteview. Accessed Octo-
    ber 5, 2021. *https://voteview.com/congress/senate*.

Underhill, Wendy. "Recall of State Officials." Recall of state
    officials. Accessed October 5, 2021. *https://www.ncsl.org/
    research/elections-and-campaigns/recall-of-state-officials.aspx*.

"US Political Conventions & Campaigns." US Political Conven-
    tions and Campaigns. Accessed October 5, 2021. *https://
    conventions.cps.neu.edu/history/conventions-in-transi-
    tion-1960-1968/*.

"Voter's Guide to Cost of College: Compare Where All the 2020
    Candidates Stand." *POLITICO,* February 20, 2020. *https://
    www.politico.com/2020-election/candidates-views-on-the-is-
    sues/education-reform/free-college/*.

"Voter's Guide to Drug Costs: Compare Where All the 2020 Can-
    didates Stand." *POLITICO,* February 12, 2020. *https://www.
    politico.com/2020-election/candidates-views-on-the-issues/
    health-care/drug-costs/*.

"Voter's Guide to Medicare for All: Compare Where All the 2020 Candidates Stand." *POLITICO,* February 26, 2020. *https://www.politico.com/2020-election/candidates-views-on-the-issues/health-care/medicare-for-all/.*

"Voter's Guide to Wealth Taxes: Compare Where All the 2020 Candidates Stand." *POLITICO,* February 20, 2020. *https://www.politico.com/2020-election/candidates-views-on-the-issues/tax-reform/wealth-taxes/.*

"Voter's Self Defense System." *Vote Smart.* Accessed October 5, 2021. *https://votesmart.org/education/presidential-primary#.YMzNEi1h2Lo.*

Wendy Underhill, Dan Diorio. "Elections and Campaigns: Primary Types." National Conference of State Legislatures. Accessed October 5, 2021. *https://www.ncsl.org/research/elections-and-campaigns/primary-types.aspx#closed.*

Wendy Underhill, et. al. Initiative and Referendum Processes. Accessed October 5, 2021. *https://www.ncsl.org/research/elections-and-campaigns/initiative-and-referendum-processes.aspx.*

Zurcher, Anthony. "US Election 2016: Bernie Sanders' and Hillary Clinton's Policies Compared." *BBC,* February 28, 2016. *https://www.bbc.com/news/election-us-2016-35666347.*

CHAPTER 14

"Ballot Return Tool." Center for Inclusive Democracy. Accessed October 5, 2021. *https://cid.usc.edu/ballotreturntool.*

"CID Ballot Tool Los Angeles County." *Center for Inclusive Democracy*, accessed October 5, 2021. *https://cavote.cidballottool.org/county.html?county=037.*

Durkee, Alison. "1 Ballot Box for 4.7 Million People: Trump Judges Reinstate Texas Limit on Drop-off Locations." *Forbes Magazine,* October 14, 2020. *https://www.forbes.com/sites/alisondurkee/2020/10/13/trump-judges-reinstate-texas-limit-on-ballot-drop-off-locations/?sh=2e8166f6c68f.*

"Overview." *Center for Inclusive Democracy.* Accessed October 5, 2021. *https://cid.usc.edu/about-us-overview.*

"Voter Location Siting Tool." *Center for Inclusive Democracy,* accessed October 5, 2021. *https://static1.squarespace.com/static/57b8c7ce15d5dbf599fb46ab/t/5ff1707c673a147f-ccba294d/1609658492916/CID+Voting+Location+Siting+Tool+-+One+Pager+2020.pdf.*

"Voting Location Siting Tool User Testimonials." *Center for Inclusive Democracy,* accessed October 5, 2021. *https://cid.usc.edu/sitingtooltestimonials.*